The Charmed Triangle

RELIGION, SCIENCE AND SPIRITUALITY
– BREAKING OUT OF BELIEF

BILL K KOUL and
VIJAY NARAIN SHANKAR

**You have to get it right first time in your life.
Understand everything as you live.**

Two modern writers speak to you to decipher the undecipherable of Karma, Destiny, science and spirituality, your messages from the Infinity, and other issues of living to complete yourself.

To life

Books last forever and, so do we. We only change shapes and forms, like our ideals, like our Creator, like those we create. Everything remains here. All we create is recycled. We too are recycled. The impermanence of everything is the only permanence.

Copyright © 2020 Vijay Narain Shankar and Bill K. Koul

ISBN: 978-1-922409-45-4
Published by Vivid Publishing
A division of Fontaine Publishing Group
P.O. Box 948, Fremantle
Western Australia 6959
www.vividpublishing.com.au

 A catalogue record for this book is available from the National Library of Australia

All rights reserved. No part of this publication may be reproduced, stored in a retrieval system or transmitted in any form or by any means, electronic, mechanical, photocopying, recording or otherwise, without the prior written permission of the copyright holder.

Contents

Preface ix
About the authors xi
Acknowledgements xiii
A brief journey — how this book created itself xv

Chapter 1 — UNDERSTANDING KARMA
The karma theory — one of the cleverest theories of humankind! 1

Chapter 2 — THE ROLE OF DESTINY
Everything around you is making up your destiny,
including yourself 17

Chapter 3 — THE RENUNCIATION SYNDROME
Turning away from life is the way of the loser 37

Chapter 4 — FORGIVE AND FORGET
Do we really, can we really, forgive? 51

Chapter 5 — SCIENCE, RELIGION AND SPIRITUALITY
The charmed triangle of our lives 65

Chapter 6 — THE TRUTH AND NOTHING BUT THE TRUTH
The truth obsession closes our minds to natural living 85

Chapter 7 — THE GOD IDEA
How we make our gods in our own image 103

Chapter 8 — WHEN OPTIMISM FAILS
Does God really do everything for the best?................................ 124

Chapter 9 — DIVINE VALIDATION — MAKING THINGS SACRED
Making things scared is our way to believe................................ 141

Chapter 10 — INTUITION AND INNER KNOWING
Messages from the Infinity for us 157

Chapter 11 — REALISTIC IDEALISM
Too many ideals get in the way of living practically 174

Chapter 12 — THE TERRIFYING QUESTION
What if the wise ones got it all wrong?.. 193

PREFACE

The Charmed Triangle: — Religion, Science and Spirituality is a collection of philosophical explorations and opinions on matters relating to life and its purposes. The authors, Vijay Narain Shankar and Bill K. Koul, are modern thinkers and writers who engage in a random but deeply thought-out discussion on a variety of concerns.

Many aspects of life have no right or wrong answers; some are embedded purely in belief systems. This work just tries to capture a few shades and perspectives about these aspects and, in doing so, it raises many more questions than it tries to answer, some due to the very nature of the topic and intrinsic mystery of life, and some questions raised deliberately.

This work is a random attempt by the authors to *decipher the indecipherable*, concepts that possibly are not meant to be deciphered in totality despite numerous past efforts made by humans — of all shapes and sizes from across the globe, of all past generations — since time immemorial. The concepts of the meaning of life, love, faith, forgiveness, God, the meaning of religion, and so on have always taunted humans.

This book is for all times, it is not subject to seasons or generations. Its contents are not intended to challenge or criticise any one person or any organisation or community in particular. In a changing world, some basic assumptions in life change too. Our understanding of our world and of our spirituality is the main one. New thinking needs courage as it cuts through beliefs.

The book is based on a series of conversations between the two authors, sitting in their respective living rooms, about 10,000 kilometres away from each other, across the Indian Ocean — one in the historical

Indian capital city of Delhi, with all its hustle and bustle and din, and the other in the quiet of Perth, a young, pristine city in Australia.

The reader is introduced to some timely radical thinking and the authors' penchant for facing reality and dealing with it with wisdom.

The authors hope this book helps the current and future generations of humans to live in a more harmonious and sustainable world, outside the silos of religious belief.

ABOUT THE AUTHORS

Vijay Narain Shankar has published over a dozen books, mainly fiction and also on culture, literature and rational spirituality. Based in New Delhi, he has been a career journalist and magazine editor, and *Imprint*.

His short stories have been widely published in Indian and international magazines and in many anthologies, as have long excerpts from his novel, *Storm in Kashmir* (2002).

His book on the iconic writer Khushwant Singh, *Khushwant Singh — In Wisdom and In Jest*, was released in 2017.

In 1965, Shankar was the youngest war correspondent in India when he covered the Indo-Pakistani war from the Jammu-Sialkot front.

He was the founding editor of *The Weekly Sun* tabloid magazine in 1977 and stayed with the magazine till 2004. He has since been writing books and often appears on television and on panel discussions. His books include the nonfiction titles *Shadow Boxing With the Gods, Gandhians in Blue Jeans, Anandpur Sahib, Shri Guru Granth Sahib* and *The Golden Temple; The Music Man*, a collection of short stories; and the poetry collections *Rusted Laughter* and *The Other Time*.

Bill K. Koul is an engineering consultant by profession and a philosopher and writer by passion. He lives in Perth, Western Australia. Bill regularly blogs on his website (https://billkkoul.com) on varied topics, including education, politics, philosophy of life, gender inequality, and life and liveability. In addition, he has been writing for various Indian newspapers and magazines. In Perth, he lectures on the history and issues of Kashmir, where he originally comes from.

Bill was born in the early 1960s in Srinagar, Kashmir. He left Kashmir in 1989 due to a socio-political uprising and lived as a refugee in India for a few years. He started working as a consulting engineer in Malaysia from early 1995 and then migrated to Australia in 1997. He has authored several nonfiction books: *22 Years — A Kashmir Story* (2017), *My Life does not have to be Unhappy* (2017), *Issues White-anting India* (2017), *Does India Need a Dictator — to Rescue a Sinking Nation?* (2018), *A Bouquet of Random Thoughts — Conversations with Myself* (2019), *The Exiled Pandits of Kashmir — Will they ever Return Home?* (2020), and *We Humans – And Our Behaviours During The COVID-19 Pandemic* (2020).

In addition to his full-time work as an engineer, Bill is working on a number of other projects, including a book which attempts to decipher the enigmatic side of humans through a compilation of real-life vignettes and anecdotes; and a book on the art and philosophy of engineering, which portrays his learning from the philosophies of both engineering and of human life in general and how they follow similar natural laws. With more than thirty-seven years of international engineering experience, Bill sees engineering as a creative art.

ACKNOWLEDGEMENTS

We must thank life and all that it is. As they say here in India, this is an opportunity, it is a custom and it is in my heart to acknowledge the gifts of people for being what they are.

I thank my wife, Brinda, and our daughters, Tanya and Lara, for their love and care through times good and not so good. It has been wonderful to be together. It is wonderful indeed when people can enrich each other's lives.

I must, at the beginning of this work, hasten to thank my co-author, Bill K. Koul, who came from the mists of a Kashmir of my childhood and youth, and became a friend in far-off Australia where he now lives. It was what we thought and what we wrote that brought us together to write the book.

There is no end to the people, the writers and the thinkers whom one should remember in such a place. They — the adventurers of the mind, in many cultures and countries, who explore and find the richest and most meaningful visions of what life is all about — are the real sages and prophets of humankind. They are deserving of respect — the philosophers and scientists and the people of wisdom — who have tried to understand and shared the human experience.

For me personally, I remember most the words of Hemingway and Hesse, Sartre and Tolstoy and Tagore and Vivekananda. But I cannot name them all, those who have gifted their thoughts and feelings to us in the magic and empathy of their writings. There used to be a saying among my elders: This is a journey of the dust. It was a reference to the mutability of the body. I once quoted this to Bill and added: 'It is also the dust that creates the mind and the consciousness. That is invaluable, for the dust blows away. What remains are the thoughts that help us live meaningfully.'

Vijay Narain Shankar, New Delhi

I acknowledge life for all its teachings. In doing so, I first acknowledge my mother, Rani (Mrs Jai Kishori Koul), and my teacher, Bhaisahib (Mr Bansi Lal Hakhu), for giving birth to my body and mind. I also acknowledge my father, Mr Jawahar Lal Koul, for exposing me to many aspects of life, as an engineer, a citizen and a son.

I acknowledge my wife, Dr Rekha Bhan Koul, our son, Baba (Dr Kongposh Koul), and daughter, Deeksha Ladakhi Koul, for exposing me to the coal-face of life which only a married man and a father can experience and without which life would never have been complete. My family has helped me to learn, grow and expand.

This book would have not been born without the inspiration and input from my esteemed co-author, Vijay Narain Shankar, who boldly shared his wisdom and learnings from life with me in this book. I acknowledge Vijay for our friendship. A geographical distance of more than 10,000 kilometres between the two of us did not stop the flow and convergence of our thoughts. A confluence of our thoughts, this book created itself in no time. Perhaps it was meant to be.

Vijay and I acknowledge our publisher, Vivid Publishing, in Perth, Western Australia, for bringing this unique book to the world. In particular, Vijay and I sincerely thank our editor, Kelly Somers for undertaking an excellent work with editing of this book that can be challenging for any reader or a reviewer.

My thoughts are quite raw and mostly my own. I am still in the process of learning and unlearning, quizzing and puzzling, wondering and pondering on this and that ... the world is amazing and so is life!

Bill K. Koul, Perth

A BRIEF JOURNEY – HOW THIS BOOK CREATED ITSELF

This book was conceived out of nothing by the authors — Vijay Narain Shankar and Bill K. Koul — during a relaxed chat, over social media, on the evening of 7 October 2019. A part of the conversation is reproduced below, which illustrates how it came about and for what purpose, and also how the title was conceived:

Bill: We are touching on extremely sensitive subjects.

Vijay: What is important is that ideas should go out to people. As I had said, they come from the Central Station. We are just receivers.

Bill: Yes, the Central Station — how they reached you and me in separate ways — only to merge again.

Vijay: Of course, it gives joy when the ideas and words come. I am happy to be the medium. So go ahead, my dear man. Or, as Aussies say, go ahead mate.

Bill: And our work won't be the final word. On every topic, we will be leaving many questions for the reader.

Vijay: Get a working title, as that gives a direction.

Bill: *Conversations on this and that* — convergent & divergent thoughts; or *Our eternal quest* — conversations on this & that.

VNS: But we need a stronger title … the *Quest* idea is good, keep that for now.

Bill: *A Random Quest to decipher the indecipherable.* We know the truth may never be cracked, we all only scratch at the surface, whether it is God or anything else. We will be like two babies trying to crack what it is all about. It is all about asking questions, leaving the reader thinking. As Socrates would say, 'I don't know'.

Vijay: Exactly. I will be radical as I think that way and with a background of past thinkers to the moderns, I think we can deconstruct a lot of assumptions. I have read and have empathy with Vivekananda and Jiddu Krishnamurti who maintained *truth is a pathless land*. The Upanishads say there are many ways to look at the truth. Freedom of thought is a way to knowledge for you must find your own way. We will have to develop a format to get all this in, without getting ponderous, or boring and academic.

Bill: Our topics and thoughts should sync with the quest of a common person — with simple language, without much jargon, except where necessary, with anecdotes, metaphors … let us target the common man and his quest.

As you said, the knowing that comes by itself when there is empathy with Nature and creation should form the basis and source of a straight, exploratory discourse, conversations — in a Socratic way — between two open-minded seekers may be the way forward.

Vijay: Great. Good luck to us. On the eve of the victory of Good over Evil, Arthur Stanley's words are worth a moment's reflection: '*The best antidote against evils of all kinds, against the evil thoughts that haunt the soul, against the needless perplexities which distract the conscience, is to keep hold of the good we have. Impure thoughts will not stand against*

A BRIEF JOURNEY – HOW THIS BOOK CREATED ITSELF

pure words and prayers and deeds. Little doubts will not avail against great certainties. Fix your affections on things above, and then you will less and less be troubled by the cares, the temptations, the troubles of things on earth.'

The first draft manuscript of this book, including all its twelve chapters, was completed on the evening of 20 December 2019, exactly seventy-four days after it was conceived. The book created itself magically, as the thoughts, received by both authors from the same Central Station, oozed incessantly from both sides and merged. This book is for all ages and for all times to come.

Chapter 1

UNDERSTANDING KARMA

The karma theory — one of the cleverest theories of humankind!

Karma is one of the unquestioned and unquestionable truths of Hinduism. For thousands of years of their history and culture, the Hindus have lived with the ancient theory of Karma that they believe explains their destinies. 'Everything that happens to each individual — good and bad — is written, inevitable,' they are told. People are made to believe their lives are controlled by their Karma, loosely defined as a divine system of reward and retribution for their actions over all their past lives.

The so-called law of Karma has controlled the Indian community for centuries and still does in this day and age of science and technology. But it is only a theory and not really validated rationally. None of us really knows if it works. The system of Karma is so pervasive in the minds of most Indians that it has also become an essential part of Buddhism, Jainism and Sikhism.

The conversation about the theory of Karma between the two authors unfolded as follows:

Vijay
I do not believe in it. It is one of the cleverest theories ever devised to explain events in people's lives and what they experience. Of course, as

always with such theories, we do not know. But no religion can accept 'we do not know'. Yet the theory of Karma has dominated the Indian mind. It is a basic belief of the Hindu caste system where humans in misery or poverty are said to have been born with bad Karma. It is also a justification for human misery and disease — for example, take my visit to Tata Cancer Hospital where I met little children with cancer. I think it is obscene to say this little child suffered for past misdeeds.

Bill
We believe in it as a fallback justice system, to reconcile our past and present miseries and to bring some solace to our bleeding, revengeful hearts, or perhaps as a wishful, rather hopeful, consolatory win in the future — as reward from the higher justice — as compensation for our past or present suffering. Otherwise how do you reconcile the tragic death of a young voluntary firefighter who lost his life whole fighting the recent Australian bushfires? He is survived by his young pregnant wife. If he was doing good Karma in the present, why did such a tragic thing had to happen?

Is Karma only for Hindus who believe in it?

Vijay
I had a rather interesting conversation with a very venerable Hindu scholar the other day, which just shows in what ways people think of Karma. With my usual penchant for questioning religious assumptions, I asked the scholar — a well-respected college professor —if it would be in the Karma scheme of things if a Hindu, a good and pious one, were to be reborn (hold your heartbeat) as a Muslim or a Christian. The old professor was at first dumbstruck and in a couple of seconds he was angry, angry as hell.

'What a terrible thing to come to your mind,' he said. 'Karma is for Hindus. And a good Hindu can only be reborn as a Hindu.'

'Is that in the Shastra or sacred books?' I teased.

Chapter 1 UNDERSTANDING KARMA

'Must be,' he said, banging his hand on the table. 'A Hindu can only be born as a Hindu.'

'So the brand doesn't change,' I said under my breath. But he heard me and his face reddened.

'Muslims and Christians do not believe in Karma or rebirth. So Karma is only for Hindus,' he confirmed with conviction. He then gave me an even dirtier look (most pious people are great at giving dirty looks) and left the coffee-house where we had met.

So how come Hindus cannot be reborn as non-Hindus? Does God or His Karma system have a separate computer or folders for separate religions? Does it mean a Hindu in India cannot be reborn as a Russian or an American or Chinese? Well, people like me will keep asking questions. And the truth is that the people who know everything … they really don't know anything.

The entire concept of Karma has dominated the Indian mind and social systems for centuries. As a result, Karma has myriad popular definitions. Karma is everywhere in the Indian way of life. As far as I go, we need to be very careful with Karma theories.

Bill

Why did you not ask him the origin of the word Hindu? You should have reminded him that it is a Greek name (perhaps around the fourth century BCE) and, thereafter, a Persian name for the people of the land of Indus (Sindhu) and, thus, the Indian subcontinent, and perhaps it did not figure anywhere — in any Hindu scripture — perhaps before Kabir or the fifteenth century. The word 'Hinduism' is itself believed to have been coined first by the British in the early nineteenth century. It certainly does not figure in any Shruti or Smriti — Vedas, Upanishads, Puraan, the Bhagwad Gita or Ramayana. So, if Hinduism is not actually a religion per se, how can it be limited to the so-called Hindus? How do we then validate the theory of Karma? Belief intertwined with sheer ignorance blinds even the scholars.

Vijay

Well, you have rightly pointed out that the word 'Hindu' is not even a word of Indian origin. But there is something else in that belief that a Hindu can only be born as a Hindu and not as a Christian or a Muslim or of another religion. And that is the isolation and insularity of Hinduism. This came in later after the Vedic period as the priestly class took over.

It is this touch-me-not isolation of Hinduism which has also divided Hindu society. It came from an obsessive sense of purity and superiority. A small example is that the Brahmins began calling themselves the Twice Born or Dwij.

The higher and lower castes could not mingle in Hinduism. This was not just the Brahmins. The high and low caste division was there. The Untouchables were considered worse than dogs and cats in the caste system. The higher caste people could pet or touch dogs but would not touch humans who were Untouchables. This touch-me-not Hinduism got broader in range with increasing contact with the West and as the foreigners (*firangis* — the white Caucasians) came here. They were called *mlechcha*, or untouchable lower ones.

It is well known that Indians who went abroad and married foreign women were excommunicated from Hindu society. I recall that an uncle of mine had gone abroad to France in the 1940s to teach Sanskrit at the Sorbonne. He was young and brilliant and married a French lady. I was in my teens in the late 1950s when this gentleman came to India with his French wife. My father had been to Oxford himself and was very liberal. He welcomed my uncle and his French wife. But no other relative in Delhi accepted or welcomed the couple. He was a Sanskrit scholar and all that, but he was married to a *mlechcha* — a lower person, not to be touched.

The excommunication ended by the late 1960s but foreigners are still, now in 2019, not allowed to enter the sanctum of the major temples. Well, I have taken a long detour to tell you that all this was

Chapter 1 UNDERSTANDING KARMA

behind that pious professor saying a Hindu could only be born as a Hindu. It was superiority, a sense of purity and looking down on others.

An unquestioned faith in Karma has produced dependence and weakness

The point is that, as you did say, Karma too is linked to faith. And those with overly traditional mindsets take things of faith to be gospel truth, which is not as it should be. Faith is a good thing but only to a point. It is a way of giving yourself strength and confidence to have faith in yourself or your god. But this complete, unquestioned faith in Karma has produced dependence and weakness. Every misery and misfortune is ascribed to Karma. And there is more. Many of our social attitudes and practices are driven by the Karma engine, the worst of them being the caste divisions. Another is a lack of compassion and spirit of helping because we say it is the Karma of the sufferer.

I recall a visit to a slum by a spiritual teacher, Sadhguru Jaggi Vasudev, a man of wisdom, I thought initially. Later, he started indulging in Indian politics. He was mortified on seeing the inhuman living conditions. He was told that it is their Karma. Sadhguru became angry on hearing this. 'It is obscene to say they suffer in a slum due to their Karma,' he said.

Something similar happened to me at the Tata Cancer Hospital in Mumbai. It was terrible and heart-wrenching to see little boys and girls, lovely children, suffering from various cancers. A senior doctor tried to comfort me, saying the smug phrase: 'It is their Karma.' His words were like barbs that wounded feelings of humanity.

I think we need to think about so many of our smug attitudes and the Karma theory, which is, after all, only a theory and has transfixed us to that smug thinking. A thinking which makes the sufferer feel guilty. I mean it is so weird.

A person who suffers does so because of something done by another body and mind — another person. Not just weird; it is cruel if it is God's justice, as Karma is made out to be in popular Hinduism.

I need hardly dwell on the Karma foundation of the worst social injustices in systems of untouchability and lower caste humans. The beautiful and humanistic philosophy of Hinduism of the Vedas and Upanishad later became the insidious monster of caste. And the basis was that a person was born lost due to Karma.

Bill
As I said, it is baffling to see even the doctors pushing the unknowns and undiscovered into the domain of Karma. It would not be surprising, therefore, that even doctors up to the nineteenth century would have termed many currently treatable diseases subject to Karma. It is true that medical science does not know everything, even now, but it is undoubtedly trying to unravel the mysteries through unrelenting scientific research. An untreatable disease which is currently brushed aside as a karmic effect may possibly be treatable after ten years. So where does Karma go?

Humans have learnt to duck away from their failures and shortcomings and hide under a cloak of Karma. It is similar to God. Anything that could not be understood in the distant past — such as rain, hail, snow, lightning or cloudburst or earthquakes — would be called an act of God. So humans created different weather gods and prayed to them.

Vijay
You have indeed pointed out something that I have often brought up in discussions on Karma. That even disease and cancers are attributed to Karma. That doctor at the Tata Cancer Hospital was not alone. We have for centuries and right up to today said that if a disease strikes, it is Karma. It is so obviously irrational and weird. We know that viruses and bacteria and cancerous cells cause these ailments. Is it even conceivable that a cancer cell or a virus would be commanded by God

or a divine power to strike a person who was immoral or who killed somebody? Are we to believe that bacteria are controlled by human and societal morals?

I would like to point out here that an American cell biologist, Dr Bruce Lipton, has worked extensively on what he describes as 'the wisdom of your cells'. He supports the theory that gene expression is influenced by environmental factors and that these factors have a greater impact than genetic research has determined previously. Lipton found that not only are there millions of cells in the human body, but also that they each have an intelligence of Nature and it seems they behave in such a way as to support growth. I found this uncanny. And the reason is simple. I recall the root of the Sanskrit word 'Brahman', the formless universal and One Supreme Power, is *Brh*, which means to grow.

I have brought this up as we have talked about disease and cells. Nature designs cells in organisms to grow and live. But Nature also designs agents to destroy those cells. It is a design of Nature. As is all life and death. Where does the retribution of Karma based on good and evil come into this?

Before I go, I must share this. I have not heard one but a number of very highly revered spiritual gurus say that diseases and illnesses are caused by beings. That is why, in the olden days, and even now, in smaller places in India, puja and mantras were recited to ask these beings (for example, for smallpox there was a devi or goddess) to go away or turn benign. So diseases were, and still are, a part of the belief system of Karma.

Bill
I'll respond to this later. I share exactly those thoughts but there are still some shades of doubt. Do we suffer solely due to our Karma? Conflicting thoughts are within me. A large part of me says it is all nonsense. We are what we do with ourselves, but then there are anomalies. Most people never make it despite their continuous efforts to survive and

succeed. Being privileged does work to an extent but not always. There is something called luck. But is it?

Vijay
Yes, do take time to think it to its logical conclusion. That's something most people do not do. And once you go into it, do something very important. Set yourself free. Cut the bonds of your conditioning. Set yourself free from what is known. Face the emptiness. The truth is where the weeds of belief and constructs of religion are not.

Yes, of course, there is luck or good fortune and bad. The most obvious thing is birth: where one is born — in a rich house or a poor house? With a brilliant mind and brilliant body? All that is never explained! And it is a determining factor in an individual's life. In Karma it is explained and in other traditions it is God's will.

I submit that sometimes in Nature there are phenomena that occur without any explanation. We seek explanations with our minds that are finite and cannot go beyond. Why that kind of birth happens is unexplained. We use the cause-and-effect theory to explain Karma and that a certain individual did good or bad. But good or bad are based on human moralities. They differ in various human traditions and societies. What is good in one is bad in another. And how do we presume that a divine person or a divine intelligence is even looking at our moralities?

There are other things — accidents, wars, natural disasters. People die and suffer in the millions. Were those things caused by the Karma of individuals? No, certainly not. World Wars I and II were not caused by the Karma of the millions who were killed. In World War II, the Karma of six million Jews could not all be on a par to all be gassed to death. These are questions that answer themselves if seen rationally. Things happen and phenomena in Nature occur due to a multiplicity of causes, some of which we do not fathom. Some of the causes are your own mind and will, then the will and minds of other people working on us, then natural causes that control your health and your senses. There are so many things and occurrences in a life, the choices you make and your ways of thinking, and not to forget your genetic make-up. All these are some causes.

But we cannot explain everything. It is the obsession to explain that creates Karma and other systems.

Bill
Well, there is something called randomness. The universe was born out of chaos. The theory of probability also works in some cases. Most things are perhaps subject to sheer chance. We try to invent stories and theories to explain those things — life and death, rich and poor. Humans want to know the reason — the 'why' and 'how' factors. In most cases, where answers are not coming from reason and rationale, we develop alternative explanations based mainly on our beliefs.

Thinking about it, the theory (or belief) of Karma plays a big role in the Hindu world. That is why it trails far behind the developed, industrialised world, where one is deemed responsible and accountable for one's actions, where people are taught 'God helps those who help themselves'. Although Karma makes us accept our failures and helps us to reconcile quickly with our grief and suffering, it does not encourage us to be more logical and strive for truth and human development through the path of rationalism or to achieve progress. It works both ways — for and against us.

I wish to share an interesting anecdote with you. The other day, I posted the following thought on my Facebook page:

'Don't waste your time in trying to know the meaning of life. Just live it the best you can — truthfully, faithfully, sincerely — both to yourself and to people you meet and interact with. Your destiny will choose you if you are meant to know the meaning of life. Life will come to you to be deciphered. It will unfold before you — extremely painful that may be — and reveal its secrets to you.

'Most of us are created — by the Creator — mainly for procreation. A few of us are meant to know why we are created. Most of us are born mainly to eat, grow, work for others, procreate, enjoy ourselves (with hedonistic happiness) and then die — and be forgotten within a generation. Only a few of us are born with an altruistic nature — with a good heart — and work in the Creator's own hands — to toil selflessly and make positive changes in the lives of people — of any caste, creed, gender, religion, region — without bias or discrimination.'

A reader responded quickly: 'I think people who never make any effort, either physically or mentally depend on others, take life very lightly, are more lucky than others.'

I replied: 'That is also an interesting perspective. I may also have met and known many such lucky individuals. Well, undoubtedly, that makes one wonder about destiny and luck — if roles and responsibilities are predestined. In any case, we all agree that a tree must endure rain, hot sun, wind, hail, snow etc. to be able to bear fruit and give it away without preconditions. That is life. Some must suffer and work for others.'

She replied: 'Mr Koul, what about their Karma, their duties and other virtues that I have never understood? They make others suffer but, as per their idiotic nature, they feel it is their birthright.'

I concluded: 'You have asked one of those extremely difficult questions and spoken about Karma! These concepts are bedded more in faith than have any evidence. Logically, we pay a price for everything; sometimes the price is paid late, but goes with interest. That is my personal belief.'

Vijay
Ah, Bill! You have said what is most pertinent here — chaos, randomness, chance. In the haste to explain and write QED on everything, our ancients and people today did not allow for the eternal mystery of our world. I recall Carl Sagan who loved his studies of the cosmos. 'The

moment we think', he wrote, 'that we have solved everything and know everything is when we would have failed.' I think Sagan was so right.

We have built up such a sure and certain iron-clad theory of Karma that we think we know all about why things happen in people's lives. I think we fail when we are so sure about how this unfathomable mystery works.

I think you have hit the proverbial nail right on the head when you mention randomness and chaos and chance. I was going to get here eventually — chaos, creation from Nothingness. We have all those theories too, now in science and before that in mythologies and in the Upanishidic philosophy. It is a vast subject, the concepts of creation from chaos. In fact, most ancient mythologies have this idea that you call randomness also. There are ancient Hindu ideas of a Supreme Being that is 'self-existent' and there is no cause in that, no hows and whys.

We can talk about that too, for I believe there is much that is self-existent in Nature (Nature to be read, when I use the word, in the occult sense of the Hindi, Sanskrit word *Prakriti*, or creative Nature). Things happen by themselves like chemical reactions and one thing becomes another.

I think this is true of humans too. Our minds and our senses are powerful energies. They drive us in various directions and to do various actions, both good and bad. I don't think we should confuse that with Karma as a law. It has been called a law by many, to underline its inevitability and rigidity. But there is no evidence of it being repeated in the same manner or pattern.

I would ask you to look at many historical and present cases of what I can only describe as Collective Karma. There are two things here:

The first is the fact that, during cataclysmic events, human-made or natural, there are very large numbers of people killed and even more of their kin who suffer. I talk of events like wars or pestilences and natural disasters. Will you think of this, Bill, as to how thousands and millions of humans have the same fate, same Karma? Where is the individual reward and retribution for one's actions in a past life or this one?

The second question I would like you to mull over is, taking the example of India, how is it that in the past and even now millions of human beings — nearly half a billion people — live in poverty and misery? Collective Karma strikes again. Why does this happen in India only and why not in Europe or Australia? Does it not point to the fact that the Karma of millions changes when practical, sound materialism takes over? Does it not seem to you that science and technology, and a practical way of life have changed lives around the world and Karma plays no role in creating misery and poverty? Once again, these are questions that I think every Hindu must ask. Why indeed is a country with so much religion so backward and defeated in giving happy lives to millions?

Bill

This is the real tough question. The answer to this question may answer many allied unanswered questions. Look, if we think about it on a relatively small scale, we will achieve a set of explanations. But then, mix some belief in with your thinking and the whole gamut changes, with an entirely different set of explanations.

I shall dig deeper and answer it later. You are now boldly challenging and shaking the common (Hindu) belief system and the mirage that we have chosen to live within. We don't even know how it all started. Was it really the Big Bang that was the origin of the universe? Scientists are not yet fully convinced about it. With each day, we keep learning about things and natural phenomena that we did not know in the past. For example, black holes.

Verily, little by little, we are knowing something about the 'big elephant' but the full form and size of this big elephant will remain unknown for a long, long time, or may never be known in full. If at all we do succeed in cracking this mystery, we may find out that it was never a big elephant that we had believed all along for thousands of years. It may turn out to be a gigantic dinosaur or perhaps nothing. We may, in fact, be probing at a beast with a toothpick. It may just be an ocean whose measure we are trying to take with a tablespoon. Remember what Newton said about being a small child playing with a few pebbles on the shores of knowledge.

If the Big Bang really happened, preceded or followed by chaos, it should not have produced anything that is predictable. Yes, we may crack a few things here and there, and on relatively much smaller scales, we will certainly keep looking at the sky — as babies — with wonder, making wishes as shooting stars pass by.

Even now, astrological predictions continue to be based on those fixed number of planets — along with *rahoo* and *ketu*, and the sun and the moon — that may have been known to the astrologers hundreds of years ago. Now you know why those predictions don't always come true? Because, in the past, astronomers and astrologers did not know about so many other stars and planets, and black holes, which have come to be known of late. If at all astrology works, those stars and planets in our solar system should logically have some effect on us. No? And then, there could be more stars, which have not yet been found. So the accuracy of astrological predictions and Karma all comes down to our ignorance.

What I am saying is there is always a reason why things happen — whether explained by astrology or not, with all its imperfections and fallacies — due to actual causation and effect. Lastly, let us remember we were just under a billion people on the planet about 400 years ago. We have grown about eight times since then and we are still growing. In the next three decades, if we escape a serious natural calamity or a nuclear catastrophe, we would have multiplied by about ten times, as another two billion humans are expected to arrive on our planet at this human production rate. A question is: 'If we are subject to reincarnation, where are these additional souls coming from?'

Some people believe we humans go through eighty-four lakh life forms before returning as humans. Some believers think some of us may have been worms, reptiles, birds and animals in our past lives. So does the Karma theory apply to those non-human life forms also? Even to invertebrates and to jellyfish too? No, that thought seems like pure rubbish.

If at all Karma theory works, humans should logically be humans in the past lives also. By the term 'human', I mean the believers (Hindus), as suggested by that scholar of Hinduism that you mentioned at the start of this chapter. For that to happen, the total number of humans (Hindus) must be constant on the planet to the last single individual. Obviously, as we have kept multiplying ourselves, this theory fails. It is not just coincidence that we humans are born as humans. Thanks to the dawn of the Industrial Age and ongoing scientific advancement, our growth has been phenomenal. But then throw in a natural calamity — an act of God, or a plague, or a global pandemic, or a major drought, or major climate change, or a nuclear catastrophe — and most of us will disappear. With that, Karma too will go out the window.

To conclude, there is no Karma. It is all cause and effect, all here and now. We come from nothing and merge into nothing. Laws of conservation of energy and matter hold good. The sum total of both energy and matter must be constant, as science says, and matter can neither be created nor destroyed. Look at the earth from outer space; it looks the same most of the time. We humans are not visible from an altitude of 10,000 feet, let alone from space or from where the Creator would be imagined (in some religions) sitting on a high chair.

Vijay
Yes, Bill, these are some very rational thoughts. I think mostly people are stuck with ideas that are said to be sacred or eternal. The Karma idea is one such. Why things happen, why people have certain experiences and so forth, will never have an answer. We must not force answers by

making things sacred. I remember the writer Khushwant Singh saying that scriptures are great thoughts of humans but nothing is sacred.

Karma, as it is popularly understood and applied, as in castes of high and low people, is open to a lot of questions.

I think what you said just now about theories like the Big Bang and other rational stuff reflects your own questioning mind, of course, but also you being an engineer, one who uses science and mathematics in his profession. Something very important in your response was that section on multiplication of population, which also means new souls coming into being. In Karma belief, there are fixed souls that move from one species to another in evolution. I liked your conclusions.

You see, Bill, everything in religion and philosophy is belief through imagination. There are theories, theories and theories. Even the soul and its existence is a theory. We feel and know emotionally, and we agree with all our being to things like love or the soul. We know with all our being. That is wisdom. But it is not the kind of knowledge that is provable or sure. It is not the knowledge that you can fight for or kill for as humans have done.

The Karma idea appeals to us and so it is widely accepted, just like many other great ideas. But we need to scan it first, along with all our assumptions, with the mind. I think we have covered some considerable ground on this. Though one is well aware that Karma, like other very deeply ingrained concepts, will be here for a long time. It will be understood by those who reflect and question, and find their way with it. But most often it will be misunderstood in popular culture.

You might well ask why I say this. Well, for the simple reason that I — and perhaps you will be of the same mind — do not want to make the mistake of being absolutely sure and locked up in my mind. It is a common and universal mistake. And it is made by most religions, which is unchanging. Science at least changes.

I see the theory of Karma as an attempt to discover. To find out the answers, humans have done this always. As we have spoken here, we find there are many questions that Karma theory answers. Let us now say that the answers are only explorations. Nothing is final or sacred.

I must share with you one of my favourite quotes from Shakespeare. It is Hamlet who speaks to his friend: 'There are more things in heaven and earth, Horatio, than are dreamt of in your philosophy.'

You see there is a whole lot of work on Karma and also books. All Indian writers and gurus accept Karma. That is unquestionable and sacred. So do all Indian gurus and my own guru Swami Vivekananda. Sri Aurobindo has done lot of work on Karma and that is interesting.

Western writers are only now beginning to question some things in the Karma theory. Deepak Chopra accepts it fully. The Dalai Lama laughed and told a writer, 'I will be out of business if I deny Karma.' Only one guru, Maa Amritananmayee, told Khushwant, 'We don't know if Karma works the way we think. But it is useful to teach morals and the importance of good deeds to common folk.'

Chapter 2

THE ROLE OF DESTINY

Everything around you is making up your destiny, including yourself

This chapter was originally titled Destiny. As thoughts started emanating, Vijay suggested this chapter be called 'Turning Away from Life' but Bill insisted the chapter be focused on Destiny, as originally intended. His reasoning was that the terms Destiny and Karma and the processes they speak of, appear to be intertwined, almost inseparably. Thus, paradoxically, Destiny demanded the chapter be focused on Destiny.

Vijay
I had thought of talking about the idea that spirituality and religion place the emphasis on non-materialism and *tyaag* — renunciation with self-sacrifice. These teachings usually devolve into hypocrisy and false piousness. My idea is also to say that all spirituality and religion must show up in one's life and character and essential goodness. Do you want to bring Destiny into it too as an additional thread? Well, it can be done! 'Turning away from life' has to be a separate chapter. It is about renunciation, withdrawal and non-materialism.

Destiny is a set of presumptions. And the God idea is central to it as God and His will (or that of a divine power) decide your fate. We do not know. It is my view that Destiny is a combination of many factors. These are causes, such as your choices and will, other people's will and actions that work on you, as well as natural and socio-political events, for example. Dr Bruce Lipton[1] says, 'Every cell in body and brain has life of its own'. As we know more through science and technology, we reject old assumptions. We may be rejecting too much. So there must be a balance between older knowledge, the wisdom of Indigenous peoples, and the new thinkers. I personally am interested in Sam Harris, Carl Sagan, Michio Kaku and Joseph Campbell (on myth and forms of life wisdom).

Harris says there is 'nothing irrational about seeking the states of mind that lie at the core of many religions. Compassion, awe, devotion and feelings of oneness are surely among the most valuable experiences a person can have.'[2] He rejects the dichotomy between rationality and spirituality, favouring a middle path that tends to preserve spirituality and science, without involving religion. He advises that spirituality should be understood in the light of scientific disciplines, such as neuroscience and psychology.[3] Harris maintains that science can show how to maximise human wellbeing but may fail to answer certain questions about the nature of being, answers to which may be discoverable directly through our own individual experience. His conception of spirituality does not involve a belief in any god.[4] Based on his experience, he recommends *Dzogchen*, a Tibetan Buddhist meditation practice, to his readers. He says the purpose of spirituality is to become aware that our sense of self is illusory, while conceding that the term 'spirituality' is used in many diverse and sometimes indefensible ways.

---

1 Bruce H. Lipton (2012) 'The Wisdom of Your Cells', https://www.brucelipton.com/resource/article/the-wisdom-your-cells, retrieved on 27 July 2020
2 Lisa Miller (2010) 'Sam Harris believes in God', *Newsweek*.
3 Peter Clothier (2016) '"Waking Up", by Sam Harris: a book review', *Huffington Post*, 2 September, retrieved 1 October 2017.
4 Holly Smith (2014) 'Waking Up: A Guide to Spirituality Without Religion', *Washington Independent Review of Books*, 17 September, retrieved 2 October 2017

Chapter 2 THE ROLE OF DESTINY

Harris says that this realisation — of self being illusory — is based on experience and is not contingent on faith; it can bring happiness and insight into the nature of consciousness.[5] He argues that science answers moral problems and can help human wellbeing.[6,7] Harris argues that the idea of free will is incoherent and 'cannot be mapped on to any conceivable reality'[8,9] and adds that 'neuroscience reveals you to be a biochemical puppet'.[10]

Bill

Is not the concept of Destiny intertwined with the concept of Karma? Thinking about it, at a conscious level, we can't even control our breath and heartbeat although experienced yoga practitioners can bring their breathing rate and heartbeat down to below-average rates.

Neither can we control the growth of our hair, finger and toe nails, or our bowel motion or sleep. These things happen outside of our conscious control. Why? The reason is that our body and body parts follow their own intelligence and biological laws, independent of our conscious control. Don't you feel that, at a conscious level, our control over our body is very superficial and limited? How much control do we really have of our individual selves? Do you really believe there is anything called free will? Can we ever experience free will? If we do, we may find that it is at a limited, and relative, level.

---

5 Smith, 'Waking Up'; *Kirkus Reviews* (2014) 'Waking Up: A Guide to Spirituality Without Religion', 29 August, retrieved 12 August 2016.

6 Katherine Don (2010) '"The moral landscape": why science should shape morality', *Salon*, 17 October.

7 Sam Harris (2010) ' The Moral Landscape', Free Press, https://samharris.org/books/the-moral-landscape/

8 Paul Pardi (2012) 'An analysis of Sam Harris' free will', *Philosophy News*, 15 May, retrieved 17 April 2016.

9 Sam Harris (2012) 'Free Will', Simon & Schuster, https://samharris.org/the-illusion-of-free-will/

10 Eddy Nahmias (2012) 'Does contemporary neuroscience support or challenge the reality of free will?' *Big Questions Online*, 13 August.

So what are we? Who are we? Are we random bubbles? Are we just our thoughts, as René Descartes suggested?

Vijay
To the Indian mind, of course, Karma alone is Destiny and there the matter ends. And that is also where the idea comes in that since Karma (or action) is what creates Destiny through an endless succession of lives, we must put a stop to Karma, or action itself. This has been the basic Hindu view. To stop Karma, one had to stop performing any action that produced a result. That would then put an end to the reward and retribution process, and to Destiny itself. It was a logical idea but I think it was narrow-minded because it did not take into account that you really cannot –— as you have said — control the smallest occurrence or episode in your own body. I have often said that in the real world of ours, it is Nature that is God. It commands and does everything and we cannot control anything, in particular, at the micro-level.

Even beyond the physical, it is Nature that influences our mind and its workings. To take a small example, a totally physical thing such as sexuality (at least we think of it as physical) can and does affect us in all sorts of ways. It interferes with our thinking and the choices we make; it affects our sense of right and wrong; it drives both mind and body to actions that we may never have done without the overpowering drive of the libido. I will stay with this example for a moment more, Bill. It is also the libido that leads to the drive of creativity and the motivation for people do great deeds of valour. I have often thought that some great writers and artists had a heightened sexuality. I think of Tolstoy and Tagore and so many others, not to forget Picasso, who shocked but delighted the world in the 1940s when he said, 'I paint with my penis'.

I go along with you in saying that we control nothing, not even our own bodies. To control Destiny or fate or what happens in our lives is a far-off thing. Having said that, there is still a thing called Destiny, or whatever happens to an individual. Having said that, people of many traditions, including the Hindus, say it is all written by a divine agency. In Christianity and Islam, it is the will of God. It is another admission that we are helpless.

There is something here that is nagging at my brain cells. It is the thought that, once again, we are trying to fill in the blanks to great mysteries with our finite intellect. We want to rush to a conclusion. Destiny is either this or that. And once again, I think it is a combination of many factors.

Ah, and then you come to free will. Philosophers have thought of this for ages. If we accept the supremacy of a god, or of the determinism of Karma, then where is the free will to do or become what we want? One way or another, everything is fixed. Let us look at the very basis of astrology, which has been practised all over the world and with a special intensity in India. The practitioner of palmistry can read your whole life's events in the lines of your palm. The astrologer reads every event from birth to death from a complicated working out of planetary positions. The tarot madam sees all that you are in the tarot cards. And there is more. There are countless other ingenious systems of foretelling.

Bill

You have logically separated free will from Destiny. With the use of palmistry and astrology or face reading or whatever tool of soothsaying, if things are prefixed, or predestined, shouldn't they be blamed for our Karma?

As for libido, some Hindus practised and professed abstinence, through a philosophy called *Hath-dharma*, which goes against human nature its very self — against the very reason how you and I and our 7.8 billion fellow humans are here on this planet, and all those trillions of humans who have existed before us. Deliberately suppressing our natural tendencies, including our sexual drive, not only goes against our nature, it is also counterproductive; it goes against the very thing we try to achieve by practising abstinence. Any kind of tendency to suppress — ourselves or others — is against Nature. It bears counter results. Imagine a world where other life forms too — flora and fauna, insects, birds, reptiles, worms — all practised abstinence? There would be no life on our planet.

It is another thing that, for the environmental sustainability of the planet itself, humans — who are endowed with a fertile brain to think and comprehend — must practise all known and proven methods to control their population, albeit without suppressing their sexual drive. Going with Nature is important.

Imbalance in natural activities results in imbalanced humans and a disturbed world equilibrium

Simply put, our conscious mind has no control on our body metabolism, catabolism and anabolism.

We have no control over our beating heart, our breath, our bowel movements, cancer cells, our libido, our appetite, our cell degeneration, our ageing process, our emotions, feelings and thoughts as well as the thoughts and behaviours of other people, weather, movements of the earth and the moon and all other stars in our solar system or the Milky Way.

We had no control over the time and place of our birth. We shall have no control, whatsoever, on the moment, mannerism and place of our death. And even then we are blamed for our Karma and our Destiny. We are blamed for everything bad that happens to us. Why? Is it just to absolve the Creator —God — of anything wrong that happens to us? Then what is God for? Is God only for taking the credit of endless human endeavour — in science and technology — in making the human life healthy, long and comfortable? Believers don't want to give any credit to humans. They say God acts through us humans. I tend to agree with them. In that case, if it is only our problem — to act responsibly and selflessly, and do all works of God — why then do we need God in the scheme of things? Is God practically only for the temples and the priests who work there, or the astrologers, palmists or gem therapists?

Why does one prostrate before God if God does not do much for us directly or make Itself visible when we want him to, especially at the times when we suffer? Do we prostrate only because of fear, lest God spoils our work or be angry at us? In essence, do we pray and symbolically prostrate before God only to keep us away from the effects of natural disasters — drought, cyclones, floods, tsunamis, earthquakes, bushfires, epidemics and so forth? Note that most of the things on the Earth, if not everything, are handled by humans. Just take a look around you — all due to science and technology.

Vijay
Bill, I am enjoying this work with you. So many things are coming up. So many contradictions in our accepted beliefs:
1. As astrology etc. mean *all is fixed*, so there is no leeway for what a person decides; and
2. A big question — if the world is *maya* or illusion, then life on Earth is also illusory, unreal. In this case, Karma and Destiny too are illusion.

I shall bring this up. I think a few passages from philosophers and writers may work. I am sharing a quote from John Steinbeck from his book *East of Eden*: 'There is a word in the Old Testament. In that passage, God tells man that all the advice has been given … now Timshel, thou mayst … decide to follow it.'

Even in the Bhagwat Gita, Krishna says to Arjuna after advising him: 'It is up to you.' That is all free will.

Bill
I still don't believe we have an absolute free will. If we had, either we were gods or dictators. The concept of free will is dangerous — it can

make a person a menacing lunatic, obsessed, a tyrant or a dictator if one is not emancipated and selfless.

I think even Jesus or Krishna did not enjoy free will. See how they operated and died. If they had free will, they could have done much more than what they are known to have actually done. They lived in the times of demons and oppressors. Free will, like democracy, is a beautiful thought. Both eventually create nuts and dictators. The concept of free will contradicts the concepts of Karma and Destiny and if things are preordained.

Vijay
Well, I think you have a point and I shall take up that part about Jesus and Krishna first. Their lives, whether mythical or real, were written by men and were meant to be in human modes or situations. And that is true of all prophets and avatars. To my mind, their lives illustrate an important aspect — that a person's life and destiny are directly influenced by other people, the situation around him and other people's will and actions. In all of this, there is a play or battle of energies and wills.

The evil Romans in the life of Christ and the demons that Krishna battled were strong forces that moulded or dominated their lives. I see them as mythologies that are the wish-fulfilment stories of humans. We want the good to destroy evil, perhaps because it does not always happen in real life. We make our gods in our own image. Then give them super powers. This is to be understood — that our life's destiny is also a play of good and evil, battle between negative and positive energies. Our myths, in all cultures, tell us we must destroy the evil because that is our wish. In real terms, I think what is happening is that good and evil are like two phases of the current. The conflict is movement, life itself.

Karma and Destiny are incomplete concepts. Interestingly, the West got out of determinism very early and progressed. The rest is still there.

I liked your candour in saying free will creates nuts if one is not really emancipated. I think free will in the true sense comes only with great wisdom. To hit somebody or conquer nations is a matter of mere physical strength.

Bill
How do we destroy 'evil'? Is evil something we don't like or are afraid of, or threatened by? Is evil something that goes, or is perceived to go, against our belief system, indoctrination, religion, community? Who decided what is 'evil'?

Should 'evil' not be our own dark side lurking within us? Is the battlefield of Kurukshetra not our own mind? Is jihad, as mentioned in the Koran, not a battle within our own selves — our dark side versus our noble side? The definition of 'evil' is something this world must revisit and revise or renounce altogether. At the moment, it is subjective. People with power misuse this term for their selfish endeavours and strategic missions.

Vijay
Yes, of course, you are right. The battlefield of Kurukshetra is our own mind. The battle is there. What you said is the crux of free will. The mind and consciousness of man is battling the evil or dark energies. You ask what is 'evil'. It is the energy of destruction, very much a part of Nature, the nature within us too. And the human mind and consciousness is fighting it because life — the positive energy — must win through. All Nature is geared to life and perpetuating life.

I think the definition of 'evil' as a destructive and dark energy is good enough. It is humans with their own moralities manufactured by them who use the word wrongly. Creation cannot take place in the evil environment. You can never destroy evil, as it is necessary, as per my analogy of negative and positive current that creates life. And both, a matter of how we balance them, create our destinies.

Bill

Despite my compelling thoughts that Destiny is a myth, there are occasions when — other than Destiny — most other explanations fail to support why a certain thing has happened. For example, the recent World Cup 2019 cricket seminal match between India and New Zealand in which India, despite being the favourites, lost the match. Strange things happened right before the toss. India made a bad team selection, dropping their strike bowler, Shami, who had earlier won them matches. Then, despite winning the toss, on a sunny day they chose to bowl, fearing demons in the wicket. However, the wicket did not turn exactly as they had expected. New Zealand saved their wickets, defended with a resolute determination and scored runs but when it looked like India was beginning to gain an upper hand, the weather god halted their winning momentum. It rained heavily and stopped the day's play. When the game resumed the next day, the sky had changed. It was cloudy and the wicket behaved differently; it helped the bowlers.

The Indian batsmen were circumspect and low on their confidence; their demons had awakened, it seemed. India lost the match against the underdogs. It seemed the Indians were destined to lose. Nothing they did worked for them. Even Nature spoiled their game.

A similar thing happened in the final match between England and Australia. All members of the Australian team, including their battle-hardened, legendary, experienced coaches, repeatedly inspected the wicket before the toss. They suspected demons in it and, contrary to the usual Australian confidence of batting first and putting runs on the board, they chose to bowl first, just like the Indians against the Kiwis. The wicket played true and England scored decent runs. The Aussies lost.

Vijay

Yes, these events are an interesting combination. But why do we presume they were events and even natural phenomena that targeted a certain team as bad Destiny? We presume because we try to find reasons. I think every event, the mistakes by the players, the weather and so forth was happening on its own, by its own causes. Why do we want to establish that Destiny or a divine force actually planned it? I think we make the mistake again in our hurry to explain. The clouds and the rain happened. Other things happened too. It is what I would call the Destiny Network of Chance. They combine to create a situation. It just happens. I seriously cannot accept that someone planned it all.

I would like to move on with you, Bill, to another aspect of our engagement with Destiny. All the ways that humans have worked out to change their life for the better — to ward off evil and bring about a good fortune — are fascinating if for nothing else but the imagination with which humans try to change 'bad' to 'good' Destiny. We are aware of the special pujas, mantras, even sacrifices that were done by the Hindus. It is common to most traditions. It was not only the Abrahamic religions that did even human sacrifice, the Hindus too had this practice in various tantric and Kali goddess cults.

Thankfully, that inhuman cruel stratagem to change Destiny has stopped in modern times. Yet sacrifices of animals continue to this day.

I once visited the Kamakhya Kali temple in Assam. It was one of the days they sacrificed goats and buffaloes as offerings to the deity. The sacrifices were made by people who paid for the animals and it was thought the sacrifice would bring good luck. It was supposed to be something holy but I can tell you it was horrible. I had to literally walk in puddles of animal blood as half a dozen buffaloes were put to the sword and sacrificed in the temple courtyard. A strange explanation was given to me by a retired college teacher from Bihar who met me at a tea shop near the temple. 'The sacrifice of living things has significance in many religions,' he said. 'Here in front of the goddess, they say there is a primal scream, unheard by us, of the dying animal. We believe that scream wakes up the goddess to help us.'

Mantras and pujas and amulets and charms exist in all religions and it is all intended to change Destiny. Implicit in this belief is that by accessing divine and/or occult forces, we can change our destinies. Indeed, the processes of changing Destiny exist everywhere and are big businesses. It is an age-old process in the East in the Islamic and Hindu traditions. The West has made it science-oriented and modern. We have things like past-life regression, the record of lives and, of course, the occult arts and Wicca cults. Witchcraft now is a trendy practice with people.

Marriage to Krishna

Be it Karma or Destiny and the inevitability of fate, humans have never given up. We have had the courage to fight and/or manipulate forces that we cannot see or know but which we imagine. All of these destiny-changers are based on fantasy, folklore and Indigenous people's knowledge. The *upaayay* or destiny-changing charms are sometimes quite logical. I'll tell you about one.

In the Hindu tradition, there are pujas and *upaayay* for all problems. I know of the mantra for solving a bad marriage of a young woman. The woman, who may have a problem with her husband, is brought to the temple. She is then ritually married either to an image of Lord Krishna or to a banyan tree. It is all done with symbolic Hindu marriage rituals. The woman goes round the idol of Krishna or the tree seven times, as is done in a real marriage. Mantras are chanted and offerings of fruit and flowers made. Then the woman puts a flower garland or *jaimala*, which signifies marriage, around Krishna's idol. The priest takes a garland from the idol of Krishna or the tree and puts it around the woman's neck. She has now been married a second time. The logic, as was explained by a priest, is that since her first marriage is going bad or is troublesome, she marries a holy or divine element, thus cancelling the original troubled marriage and invoking the divine into her symbolic second marriage.

Chapter 2 THE ROLE OF DESTINY

I thought that was very logical and ingenious. Does it work? Well, at best, one can say it creates a positivity and new hope. That is not inconsequential or trivial. You might well laugh at me for this. But I think there, in a positive energy being created, is a strong auto suggestion and motivation for self-belief. These are transformational, as effective as advice from a psychiatrist.

Let me give you the best and biggest example I know about the transformational power of auto suggestion and positive motivation.

I have written three books on Sikhism, as it is a faith that interests me. It is a modern faith, only about 500 years old. It was a faith established by a village dweller in Punjab as a reform to the ritual-bound, older Hindu faith. To put it briefly, the Hindus there suffered conquests and oppression at the hands of Muslim conquerors and rulers. Weakened by their beliefs and social divisions, the Hindus were helpless and lived as slaves. Their spirit was broken. Guru Nanak started a simple faith of devotion to a Supreme Being and cut out rituals and beliefs that weakened people. The ten gurus who followed him began to resist the Mughal armies as guerrilla warriors.

The tenth guru, Guru Gobind Singh, established the Sikh faith with sword in hand and developed the Sikhs into a martial race. The same weak, miserable, defeated Hindus, motivated by the gurus to go fearless and feel proud, became great fighters and are known even today to be great achievers. I find this historical sudden turnaround of people a little apocryphal although it is possible that people would have been transformed gradually and their Destiny changed.

Bill

Why does Destiny have to be intertwined with Divinity? Why does everything have to be routed back to Divinity? Can we redefine Destiny independent of Karma and God? For example, to say it is a logical chain of events which just leads up to something happening, like luck, like lottery, based on probability — just being at the right place at the right time — as a matter of chance, pure coincidence, random chance. Can't random chance be considered as Destiny?

Perhaps Destiny is pure luck — good and bad — just a matter of chance. Perhaps, it has all happened already and we are just catching up with time. There is an old English saying: *The coming events cast their shadows before.*

When a die is rolled, one out of six numbers comes up. Does that mean a particular number will come up in six attempts? Yes and no, both. It is actually a matter of chance. Is Destiny also a matter of chance? Do we say the realisation of those chances which have the least probability of happening is caused by Destiny, or not? I think we ascribe Destiny to mainly those events that have the least probability of occurring.

Vijay

Of course, you are right that we force ourselves to believe that God and divine powers are involved in our Destiny. I go along with you that it is all a series of events happening coincidentally to produce a certain result. In fact, the Buddhists and others do not believe in God, but they still believe there is Destiny. For the Buddhists, our Destiny is based on our Karma. They believe in Karma and rebirth.

Einstein, a great man, said he did not believe that a god was involved in the lives and destinies of each human and all life forms. He believed in the pantheistic god of Spinoza, who said there were inbuilt laws in Nature and they caused events. Randomness and chance or just luck, things happening by their individual causes and laws, all this creates events in our lives. I would go along with that.

As I have been saying, we can and we do give direction to our lives by our will and the choices we make. I look at my own life and you can look at yours. We made certain choices in our lives. Everyone does. Sometimes they work out, sometimes they don't. There is a whole Destiny Network of many causes at work — unrelated events and

Chapter 2 THE ROLE OF DESTINY

many people and their will and attitudes towards us. I think we just call it Destiny or fate or luck to explain it.

Let us look at it in the larger picture of events that take place in the universe, the stars and planets. Or look at events in Nature, the life in the oceans. Everything is causing everything else. Natural events are taking place every moment. So is it with us? We have to accept the responsibility and find our own place. Some events we cannot control. They happen by the sheer chance of where we are placed in life, like birth or parentage and genetic factors. There are other things in our lives that we can control and choose to do. We don't know how they will turn out. I suppose that is good or bad luck for us. It is like the die you mention. We don't know how it will fall. But the die falls in a certain way propelled by its own movement. We have been trying since forever to figure it out. And we don't know still and call it fate or Destiny.

Well, Bill, I guess that is good for today. I think it is a good going, you have to admit it. Bill, you may take a look at the following suggestion I am making ... I myself do not understand it well enough. I am sure you will — that pure mathematics expresses much of the patterns of randomness and chance, how events are self-existent.

Ramanujam, the Indian mathematical genius, once said: 'My equations are worthless if they do not express a thought of God.' I find it interesting. If you feel like it, you might take it up.

Bill

I love your explanation to the points I raised earlier — solid explanation. So am I right in saying that there is something called Destiny, which is subject to some cause and effect and some to chance — subject to the law of probability and some to total randomness? Am I right in saying that Destiny, as understood in a traditional sense, is not necessarily a product of divine will or Karma, or perhaps is — if the definitions of God and Karma are revisited and re-formed — based on logic, and not solely based on belief.

Perhaps, as we will discuss later in the relevant chapters of this book, if we revisit the God concept and Divinity — based on evidence and the secrets revealed by God's Creation — of this world, and its physical laws within the scientific domain, everything makes sense. We may then be able to defend both the theories of Karma and Destiny.

I believe it is all related to the starting point. If our starting point is embedded in a belief system, then all these concepts — Karma and Destiny — too appear belief-related, which does not satisfy some rational minds like us. However, most other people — educated or uneducated — who have faith in their belief systems, have no issues with them. They find all explanations, real or imaginary, to defend their beliefs.

If we manage to shift the goal posts and tweak our perspectives, based on what is actually proven and known about the world we live in, these theories may fall into place, or perhaps not. What I am trying to do is to wrest a little control back to us poor mortals and not resign to a hopeless thought that we don't exist in the bigger scheme of things — the Higher Design.

Take an example of a soap bubble. Its strength, size, direction and life depend on all laws of physics and chemistry: the viscosity of the soap solution, surface tension, the quantum of force used to whip the soap solution, the force with which it is blown away, the natural wind direction(s), atmospheric pressure and temperature, and perhaps several other factors. And that is all known. But that is not all. There is also a factor of the unknown, completely unrelated to the bubble itself, that dictates its fate. Suddenly, a child appears from nowhere, notices it and tries to catch it, thus killing it. Now, how do we define and describe this little hand of a child?

Let us take another example. Let us talk cricket, my favourite religion. Traditional copybook batsmen, for example Rahul Dravid, have a limited, copybook, range of playing a certain type of a delivery. Here comes Steve Smith. With his sharp eye and a rapid movement

Chapter 2 THE ROLE OF DESTINY

of his feet, he can change the fate of any delivery. Bowlers don't have much clue about how to bowl to him. With his unpredictable body, leg and feet movements, he changes his stance within the fraction of a moment and chooses to play as he decides to play — on the onside or on the offside. Here we have an excellent example of a person who does not accept what is thrown to him, he exercises his choice and makes his own Destiny. Remember Steve entered the Aussie team as a bowling all-rounder and started at number 9 or 10.

He worked his way upwards through determination and hard work. There is a method in his madness and he was worked very hard, thought very hard and practised in the nets his method of madness. He is the current number one batsman in Australia and among the top batsmen in the world, and acknowledged only second to the legendary Sir Don Bradman.

Take another example. We are currently experiencing a low-pressure system over Perth. Since yesterday afternoon, we have had rain with wind. It has rained overnight and continued to rain till early this morning. Looking at the weather forecast in my weather app and hearing rough weather outside (as it is still dark outside), I should not have ventured out for my regular early-morning run. But I did. As soon as I stepped out, the conditions changed, albeit temporarily. I saw some blue patches of the sky overhead and sunrise over the river to the east, marking a near-perfect morning. As soon as I completed my morning run of six kilometres, the predicted rough weather returned. Fortune favours the brave, as they say. I was lucky to have a thirty-minute window to complete my running ritual. Interestingly, except two other brave individuals, I did not see any other regular morning walkers or runners on this very popular track during those thirty minutes of my run. Normally, hundreds of morning walkers and runners use the track at this time of the day.

Now, is it a matter of choice, Destiny, fate, luck, Karma or bravery, or none or all? I don't know. I simply took a decision against the odds —

as I usually do — and stepped out. At times, I have also gotten heavily drenched to the bone but I have never stopped once I step outside my home. Determination makes the difference!

Once I was a witness to a conversation between a senior colleague at REC Srinagar, a professor with a PhD in civil engineering, who had been my teacher at undergraduate level, and the legendary Pandit Prem Nath Shastri, a renowned pundit of Hindu Shastra and astrologer. The professor asked the pundit, 'Maharaj, what is *saath* (*mahurat*)?' The wise pundit replied: 'When a person is determined to accomplish anything that is *saath*. Unshakeable sheer determination is *saath*.' We have an illustrious scholar of religious scripture, a noted astrologer, saying our determination is our *mahurat*. Obviously, he believed in the human endeavour much more than anything else.

To end this chat on Destiny, in the first innings of the second Ashes test against England in 2019, Steve Smith faced ferocious English bowlers and was hit many times on his body. When he was batting at 79 runs, he fell to the ground after being hit awkwardly on his head. He suffered concussion but stood after some time and was later taken off the ground, visibly shaken, for a medical check-up. Against all expectations, after some time he returned to the middle and resumed his innings. After hitting a couple of classic boundary shots, he was out, obviously still shaken from his injury. On medical advice, he rested for the next test. When he returned in the fourth test, he scored a double century and continued piling runs. Determination to stand, face your adversary and not give in defines Steve.

A person of strong faith and belief will ask: 'Who is giving Steve his determination?' By *who*, the person will make a subtle hint towards God. This is because God is credited with everything good you do or that happens to you but never blamed for your misfortunes and sufferings, for which your Karma and Destiny are to be blamed.

Chapter 2 THE ROLE OF DESTINY

Vijay

Wonderful to read your thoughts after your walk! I had written something to you before your run. Nice to see how a good night's sleep brings clarity. In my own case, it is a good night's sleeplessness that seems to open up the mind. Here it is. I loved the reply of that gentleman about the *mahurat* — auspicious time to do something. I think you have said it all now in a conclusion which does not put the lock on new thought about Destiny and Karma and the mysteries we live with. I think that is the only way to go — to question what is known or is believed, not with arrogance, but with humility; to be able to look at and perhaps accept new ideas. We need to be rational, of course, and we do have the touchstone of reason and logic.

We also have imagination and an expansive consciousness. Because of that, belief and mythology become metaphors. They are metaphors for what is not fully known but what we think can be or should be. That helps us in many ways to live. But I always recall what the philosopher Joseph Campbell said, that if we take metaphors to be real or factual, we have a problem. So I do think there is wisdom in questioning and seeking evidence, and also having beliefs with the awareness that they are beliefs.

Bill

To conclude, while Karma and Destiny may work in practice to help some of us in dealing with our ill luck — but only to the extent it is the result of the law of probability — and reconciling with our misfortunes over which we may have absolutely no control, both concepts actually work against our progress and evolution. Where our full and sincere endeavours could make a significant positive difference in our lives and others too, many of us hide behind them. Both concepts annoyingly provide us with avenues to escape from our responsibilities and accountabilities. The tendency to shove our responsibilities under the carpet not only undermines our social consciousness and proactive citizenship, but it also costs the world dearly. Belief in Karma and Destiny, or the absence of it, seems to have set the developed world apart from the developing world. In the former, people generally believe in creating their own Destiny through their sustained, determined efforts, while in the latter world, people accept their miseries as their Destiny, as a result of their past Karma. People tend to live less in the present world and more in their past life that they know nothing about; they miss out on their actions in the present world (the actual Karma), which could change their Destiny in this life.

Chapter 3

THE RENUNCIATION SYNDROME

Turning away from life is the way of the loser

In the Indian context, spirituality and religion place the emphasis on non-materialism and *tyaag* — renunciation with self-sacrifice. This usually becomes a hypocrisy and false piousness. The idea here also is to say that all spirituality and religion must show up in one's life and character and essential goodness.

Vijay
This is a topic where I go against the mainstream. I oppose renunciation and withdrawal. I speak for life — a good, well-lived, humane life, of high values. There is a Zen saying that says a lot more than it seems to: *Water that is too pure has no fish, no life.* It applies perfectly to spirituality and the quest for something 'higher' or salvation that has engaged the minds of humans for ages. What this sentence from the Zen tradition tells us is that a highly sanitised spirituality, cloistered in the protective folds of renunciation and isolation from the world, is barren. It has no connect with life. Nothing grows there in the perfection of extreme denial. Well, it is a point of view.

To renounce, to withdraw from the desires and passions of living, to go into modes of asceticism, these are ideas that dominate in all religious traditions. More or less, Hinduism and Buddhism, perhaps because they grow from the same root, placed the highest importance on renunciation, the turning away from life. There is less of it in Christianity and Islam, though there have been and still are cults of extreme asceticism, even self-torture. The Abrahamic religions too give great value to intense religious practice and denial of worldly concerns.

For most of us who want to live in the best way we can, it is important to understand and have a position on how life is to be lived. There are some questions that come to us in quiet moments. Is it necessary in the spiritual path to deny all or most of physical material life? Are renunciation and asceticism the only way to find salvation? Many more such questions come up. In most cases, there are standard and timeworn answers, because our religions have worked out all the answers. But have they, really?

Shouldn't one walk alone?

Well, Bill, with the kind of thinking I have on this, I really do feel I walk alone. I think you will recall those wonderful lines by Tagore: 'When no one walks with you, then you must walk alone.' One is a bit alone when going against the tide. I do not believe that it is either necessary or even desirable to renounce the world in the spiritual quest. For one thing, to turn away from all that we have in our lives would be darn uncomfortable. I am not being facetious. I do believe in the natural synergy of the mind and body. They work together and live together and die together. If your body is protesting with pain or hunger or sickness, my simple view is that it would be extremely difficult to get on to spiritual things. There is just too much separation of the mind and body, of material and spiritual life.

That is the first thing to be understood. It is as if a person is supposed to live a double life: one of religion and spiritualism and the other of worldly materialism.

Chapter 3 THE RENUNCIATION SYNDROME

Why should one ride two horses?

There was a time when this dichotomy was stated by thinkers and writers in a telltale form. They came up with the phrase: *The ghost in the machine.*

This meant the body, the physical system we have, was a machine that could do things and move, while the mind or soul or consciousness was the ghost inside that drove it. I just have to say it does not work that way. We have lived with this separation for centuries and it is a kind of half and half life. You end up with a confusing, schizophrenic spirituality. What I mean by this is that people have lived half this and half that.

Ordinary people, who are not ascetics, have to live and work. Then they think they have to be religious in another compartment, which is like riding two horses. This is so true that it hurts. This view of a double life has really impacted the world in strong ways. The ones who have most obviously taken this up are the renouncers — the priests and ascetics, and the monks and, of course, India's millions of sadhus. I am quite aware and do accept that some among these people have attained a high spiritual level and have perhaps completed their quest. But these people are few.

The majority have certainly loved the life they did choose and yet they, and we, have no way of knowing whether spiritual evolution did take place. I will probably be crucified for saying so. Because how do you sit in judgement over anybody's religious or spiritual progress? You really cannot, I concede. These people seeking salvation, *Moksha* (freedom from the cycle of birth, death and rebirth) and *Nirvana* don the robes of renunciation and practise prescribed austerities. Nobody will ever know where they have got to.

But I have a simple yardstick. I assert that a person's spiritual state of evolution and their religious values must show in his or her life — in the kindness, universal love, compassion and humanity that the person lives with in daily life. It must manifest in his or her behaviour, temperament and actions.

Renunciates and sadhus of India

I will take a moment to talk about the sadhus or ascetics of India. We have four to five million sadhus. The word 'sadhu' comes from *sadhak* (seeker) and *sadhana* (the practices and struggle to seek enlightenment). We have hundreds, if not thousands, of cults, ashrams (places of reclusive practices) and religious centres, called *muths*, in India. There is a major concentration of these on some ancient holy pilgrimage towns on the banks of the River Ganges. In big towns, like Hardwar, Varanasi and Rishikesh alone, there are nearly three million sadhus. Most of them are celibate and renunciates, generally clad in saffron-coloured clothing. There are very large numbers of *Naga* sadhus who wear nothing at all, except that they are smeared with ashes. It has been a grand tradition of India. They own nothing much beyond their clothes and do not participate in worldly life. They are also respected by common people.

There is another side to it. Large numbers of people, usually illiterate or semi-literate, cannot find work or a way to live, or have become dropouts. Many of them head for the holy pilgrimage centres where they become sadhus. Unemployment, lack of education and no social security leads a sizeable percentage of people to become sadhus. This must not be read as a generalisation. It is not meant to be. The point I raise here is that, in a country with a huge amount of unemployment and no social welfare for the underprivileged, it is not surprising that religion becomes a support for them. In fact, to go further briefly on this, religion has been one of the biggest sources of income and occupation and economic succour to large numbers of people.

So, then, we come to the crux of this — that very large sections of the Hindu population, as well as people in other traditions, are

Chapter 3 THE RENUNCIATION SYNDROME

renunciates and clad in robes because it is a way to live. They live in disciplines of religious practices and are pious in some manner, yet it is a way of living they have chosen; the spiritual aspect is a question mark. Everything for them, and for others whose lives are filled with pious practices, is ritual, observance of certain taboos and adherence to rigid dogma of their cults and organisations.

People who renounce or abandon or drop out of the material world also abandon work and a productive life in society. This is an aspect often brought up. And it does raise an important issue. The renunciates must live in a material world where everything is to be done by others. Everything is to be produced by others. The millions of renunciates in India do no work. It is the same everywhere. This is something that has to be considered.

Bill
Please maintain your flow. I don't think we should break it. Deep rivers flow long distances. You are one such deep river.

Vijay
Haha! I brought up the sadhus and other full or partial renunciates because this whole concept of turning away from the world so as to go into religion and spiritualism is such a big aspect of many cultures. Of course, there is much less of it in the Western world. I have never been reconciled to the matter of renunciation. This is especially so when such a thing happens in the middle or later years of a person's life. By that time, there is a family and responsibilities. Of course, there is also responsibility to play one's role in society, which is flouted.

The poor and unemployed either become sadhus or live in families or on charity, having announced that they are holy men. There are also the rich who turn into ardent devotees of a godman or a godwoman and who are legion in India. They are encouraged by their gurus to renounce desire and wealth, and their wealth is usually gifted or willed to the guru and his or her religious organisation. This is not all. Due to strong cultural conditioning, it is considered noble and high-minded to 'give up' and relinquish all desire, passion, ambition. The goal for everyone is *Moksha* and it is great to think and talk about it.

What I am finally getting at is a bit of a spanner in this religious and spiritual carnival. Whether in India, where we are coming from, or elsewhere in the world, where Hindu and Buddhist traditions of spirituality are becoming increasingly popular, it has to be understood that renunciation is not a mass movement. It cannot be and never has been one. Let us look at this for a moment.

It is my firm belief that all, or most, of us need a certain amount of religion and spiritual elevation. They are a part of our lives, which must be lived in the world with all that living entails — the joys and sorrows, struggles and achievements, and all the experiences that come our way. We cannot all become obsessive spiritual persons. In any case, the obsessive religious person is usually a fanatic.

The dedicated religious life has always been thought of as a 'calling'. It is still so. It is a gift and a tendency, like painting or poetry or playing music. That is the only way it works. Mass religion and the huge followings of gurus and godmen or godwomen are suspect, in my view, as far as real, deep-down spirituality goes.

I cannot but share what the famous Indian writer Khushwant Singh once said: 'The temples and ashrams and religious functions are the gymkhana clubs of the middle classes.'

Do we live in two worlds?

There is, I must point out to you, such a thing as an ersatz religiosity. It is there but it is self-induced, built up. The whole idea of abandoning worldly life is never meant to be an option for the masses. I do not think it is necessary, even in those who wish to and can attain the highest spiritual awakening.

Chapter 3 THE RENUNCIATION SYNDROME

This is best underlined by the life of the sixth guru of the Sikhs, Guru Hargobind Singh (1595–1644). By the time he became the guru of the entire Sikh community, in the seventeenth century, there was conflict and oppression under the Mughal rulers. Guru Hargobind Singh saw all this and decided that religious leadership was not enough. The guru then decided to wear two swords on either side. He announced that one sword was for *Piri* (religious leadership or spiritual power) and the other sword was for *Miri* (temporal leadership, worldly power). I have always thought that was the right way. We live in both worlds.

Bill
Vijay, I recall my esteemed spiritual mentor, Sri Bansi Lal Hakhu (Bhaisahib), a teacher of Transcendental Meditation and a direct student of Maharishi Mahesh Yogi, saying: *Give a dog a bone*. He would say this in the context of *upwas* (fasting) as a religious ritual. He would never observe a fast. Being a teacher of meditation, he believed in a balanced life where the mind is not distracted by any *hathyog* (the physical exercises of yoga), such as fasting, celibacy, asceticism or renunciation. He would question if your belly and mind — through your five senses (sight, smell, taste, hearing and physical touch) — was craving food (a metaphor) for survival or otherwise. How can you justify fasting because it requires you, or is aimed to, to have a settled mind and closeness with your *üp* — consciousness? He believed any force applied on the body and mind, through all those commonly known methods of *hathyog*, were counterproductive and really did not help one to achieve the intended objectives of the *hathyog*. And I agree with him, absolutely.

A materially balanced and satisfied body is important for a balanced mind. For that matter, in most aspects of life, mind and body affect each other. As a matter of fact, it is not very easy to say which one affects the other more; it is like a chicken and egg question.

However, let us look at this problem logically. When a child is born, what gets activated first in the child — body or mind? I think it is the child's body. Physical hunger, pain, discomfort and so on all creep in immediately after the child's birth. The child generally functions instinctively. It is only after a few months or even years that the child's mind starts playing an equally dominant role. That is, even when the child is not really hungry, the child's mind craves his or her favourite food — ice cream, chocolate, *laddoo*, candies or sweetened beverages, for example.

Gradually, as the child grows, his or her mind starts playing tricks and corrupting their body: greed sets in. The child lies and acts to get what their five senses, and not necessarily their belly, wants. As an adult, most of the person's demands are generated by his or her dissatisfied mind — generated by greed, lust, desire, cravings and urges to possess — and not really his or her physical body.

Therefore, how can one settle his or her mind? By making themselves physically devoid of physical wants and cravings? No, not at all, as that will exacerbate the cravings and distract the person away from balance, possibly push them down the food tree. A reasonably satisfied body — in moderate quantities — is essential for a satisfied mind. That is how I think, although the process later on becomes much more reciprocal, that is a degree of interdependence of the wants of the body and the wants of the mind sets in.

I believe the body must not be troubled unnecessarily if one intends to settle one's mind. Therefore, personally, I don't believe in the *hathyog* or any forced renunciation (*tyaag*) or anything which goes against basic human nature.

Humans, like other animals, have physical wants: food, clothes, shelter, sex, comfort and so on. So, metaphorically, why keep the dog hungry? Give the dog a bone to keep busy and you do what you need to do to achieve a settled state of mind and to live a well-balanced life.

In the previous chapter, I commented on people practising and calling for celibacy through abstinence — a form of *hathyog* — which

I believe goes against the very creation of this universe and human nature itself. Deliberately suppressing our nature and natural impulses is seen to be counterproductive, bearing counter results. Going against our nature causes an imbalance in natural processes and produces imbalanced humans and an unstable world.

Vijay
Your response is very nicely explained. Tomorrow, I will respond to this body–mind theme that you introduced.

Bill
Good morning, Vijay. Today is Saturday. I am sitting by the river. This tree in front of me reminds me of you. This tree is nourished by the river flowing adjacent to it and the sun above, both helping it to go deeper and grow larger. I enjoyed reading your posts from yesterday again and I am a hundred percent in concurrence with you. I also read your thoughts to my wife, Rekha, while we were walking by the riverside. Rekha has compared the Zen wisdom of pure water with the practical uselessness of pure, 24-carat, gold, which is relatively very soft and deforms easily. An ornament made with 24-carat gold quickly loses its shape and utility. That is why a few carats of copper or silver are added to it to make it strong and durable. She also said if a person really wanted to achieve detachment or spiritual elevation, there may not be one way but numerous ways to do so. One solution may not, and does not, always fit all.

In the traditional Indian system, *sanyas* meant more of an ascetic or a detached lifestyle, prescribed for a person between the ages of fifty and seventy-five, after which — if one survived — the person was expected to leave their home and family life and move into the *Vaanprasat* ashram somewhere in a remote forest, till death. But, practically, in the past, how many people really lived up to fifty, let alone seventy-five?

As such, family life in the *Grahastya* ashram — prescribed between the ages of twenty-five and fifty years — was considered the toughest. The thinking seems to suggest that family life is difficult, filled with drudgery, and that one cannot really enjoy it. This thought promotes an escapist tendency from life, with its pleasures and struggles. It is a total denial of the life process. No wonder the world was called a *maya* (an illusion), with one biding one's time here on the Earth as if it was a prison.

It appears, designed with an escapist mindset, the 25-year *sanyasi* period was to prepare the person, mentally and spiritually, for a more disconnected and detached existence, away from the real physical world, in the *Vaanprasat* ashram. It seems the focus was to prepare the person for his or her final moment of death and detachment from material life prior to that. Sadly, it seems it was also a process of escaping from life and not really living it full till one's end. Were the people, those who would live beyond fifty, supposed to just exist and think only about the afterlife, which nobody has seen?

Now, let me sum it up. There are all kinds of individuals. Some choose the path of asceticism and renunciation as a means of escapism from life and the real world where you have to work and battle hard, as a student or a worker or as a responsible member of a family, community or the broader world. Such people generally feed on the fruits of hard work done by others. Some are also misled and brainwashed to adopt the path of renunciation. Some are naturally withdrawn from the material world. They are indisposed to a more private, withdrawn, detached spiritual life. Many of them still choose to live a normal, responsible, material life. And some individuals — based on their consistent life experiences — become naturally withdrawn and detached, and voluntarily decide to adopt the path of renunciation.

My biggest question is: if we are born in this world complete with all our faculties and hardly knowing anything beyond this physical world of ours, what is the need to follow illusions and escape from the world that exists right before us, in front of our eyes? One can still detach oneself from the toxicity of the material world based on contemplation; a deeper philosophical understanding of the reality of this physical world and its laws; or self-discipline, discretion, prudence and pragmatism. We can still lead the life of a *sanyasi* yet operate as a CEO and be of some use to those numerous souls who are also connected to the same Central Station as us. *Let us live like lotus in a muddy pond.*

Vijay
Good morning, Bill. The above statement from you and the gold analogy by Rekha is absolutely wonderful. It is so true. I think you have put it very nicely and with a telling simplicity. I also wish there were more wise people like the guru and spiritual teacher you mention. Most gurus and godmen today repeat centuries-old ideas.

Everything old is deemed sacred and so becomes infallible. It is a pity because what is sacred becomes an impediment to thought and philosophy in the present.

If we understand well what your guru was saying, about the irrelevance of empty ritual, we would know that it is the essence of the awakening of the best in us, which is of importance. Everything is just activity; doing that instead of this.

You are so right when you talk about the stress of austerities and fasting and following rules of purity. There is a tremendous amount of anxiety and stress. I know of a person with diabetes who collapsed with low sugar as he insisted on fasting. He was given a drip. On regaining consciousness, he was very angry and claimed God would not forgive him. I said with brutal frankness that I did not think God would even notice.

If the body is in stress due to fasting or renouncing certain things, it is going to pull at the mind. Then we achieve nothing.

I agree entirely that body and mind work together. Medical science now also tells us this. What we think is physical and gross actually creates the subtle and spiritual. That is self-evident. Without the physical backup of life and body cells and functioning organs, the mind and the consciousness cannot exist. There are practices of meditation and also *hathyog* which I see as preparatory activities, just as a gymnast prepares their body. I may also concede that the preparation can be beneficial to a person. But, by themselves, these things have nothing to do with spiritual awakening.

I think you have noticed, Bill, that I am perhaps using the word 'renunciation' here in its widest sense of not only turning into ascetics, sadhus and monks, but also a mental idea of renunciation or leaving the world, abandoning worldly life. This mental idea of 'leaving it all' has become a core theme for people who get into the spiritual stream in a big way. This really brings us to what we talked about earlier — the separation of religious life from worldly life.

I will only say in passing that this separation has produced a strange result. Very religious people have also been extremely aggressive, violent and cruel people. Not just kings and religious leaders, but also ordinary people who are obsessed with the supremacy of their religion. I think it was the writer Umberto Eco who remarked, 'People are never more evil and cruel as when they do it for a good cause.'

What is important is awakening. What is important is living to human completeness, the idea of perfection. What is important is not what you do but what you think — the example of *maa* that, during *bhajans*, one should be living in the moment and not be elsewhere. The abandonment and ecstasy transports you for some time. You actually turn away and are out of the world for some moments. Epiphany or ecstasy is an experience of momentary elevation. I do not think bliss on the sense of permanent resentfulness and stillness is either possible or required. It would be very boring.

As an ending, at the last of the discussion, we may use this lovely quote from Rabindranath Tagore: 'Deliverance is not for me in renunciation. I feel the embrace of freedom in a thousand bonds of delight.'

Chapter 3 THE RENUNCIATION SYNDROME

I looked at the picture of the tree again, the one you sent today. A beautiful thought from you, I would want nothing more than to be that.

Bill
I am once again in complete concurrence with you. There is an anecdote about my guru. It happened about twenty-seven years ago. Those days we lived on a fish farm in Jammu, open and all green, on the banks of River Tawi, with beautiful trees and fish ponds — all developed by my father. We Kashmiri Pandits were recent refugees from Kashmir at that time.

My teacher (guru) announced the wedding of his younger son. Since we had this privileged facility at the fish farm, my parents requested him to perform the wedding ceremonies, over about a period of one week, at our place.

One morning, after I stepped out of my bedroom — still 'dirty' as all the toilets were busy — I sat outside the house, not far from where a puja was being performed by a priest. My teacher asked me to sit near the *agni* (scared fire) and participate in the puja. I said to him that I could not do so as I was still 'dirty'. He gently smiled at me, with love in his eyes, and firmly ordered, 'Billu, go there and sit in the puja. You don't need to clean yourself; your mind is clean.' I complied and wondered about his judgement.

Another anecdote to share: between 1991 and 1994, we used to have many guests — recent Kashmiri Pandit refugees, our relatives and friends — visiting us and some living with us for weeks, sometimes months together. So Rekha would not be able to take shower before 10am. Because of that, she could not meditate regularly on most mornings. One day, Bhaisahib — the guru — asked her why she did not meditate regularly, as he could tell a lot about a person right from looking at one's face. She apologised and offered the excuse of guests occupying the bathroom in the mornings, to which he advised: 'As soon as you wake up, sit up in your bed and meditate. There is no need to wash yourself before meditating if that does not happen every day due to the reasons you have given. The purpose is to meditate regularly and settle your mind. Rest, everything is secondary.'

Vijay
Your teacher was a great man! A truly wise man!

Chapter 4

FORGIVE AND FORGET

Do we really, can we really, forgive?

Do we really, or can we really, forgive? We are told in many different ways that it is important and good and emotionally beneficial for us to be able to forgive those who hurt us.

While it is in human nature to seek justice for what causes us pain and sorrow, it is also true that the pursuit of revenge becomes a toxic and harmful burden. So in some way that one must work out for oneself, it is important that we deal with the natural urge for continued anger and revenge so that we can live our lives without being chained to anger and hate.

Even if there is not total forgiveness, it is possible to work around your actual instinct and to put some of the anger aside so that you can get on with life.

Bill

The mistakes made by us inadvertently may not possibly stain our innocence. To err is human, we may deserve forgiveness. But when we knowingly commit actions that bring misery to many people, what do we expect for ourselves? Do we still deserve forgiveness?

Vijay
It is impossible to forgive fully and totally. Everything that happens to any of us leaves behind its scars, whether it is physical hurt or an emotional episode of pain. Natural memory will keep coming up whether we like it or not. What I am saying is that it is not always an act of will to be able to forgive or to forget.

But I also do think that, at certain levels of religious or spiritual realisation, it is possible to forgive, if you believe that God and Nature will somehow restore the balance. I mean we say God will take care or Karma will punish. There are two takes on this: one is that we get out of the way and, with a heightened sense of nobility and belief, we say 'we forgive'. But the second take is that, in reality, we don't want to forgive; instead we expect God or Karma to punish the person.

The case of Australian missionary Graham Staines (1941–1999) comes to mind. He and his two pre-teen sons were sleeping in a van parked out in the garden as it was too hot inside their house, which was without electricity. A gang of religious extremists killed all three of them that night. They chained the doors of the van and set it on fire. Afterwards, his wife, Gladys Staines, left India. But before she left, she said she had forgiven the murder accused, Dara Singh, who had led the gang of murderers. I have never understood how she could forgive them, perhaps my failing. Though I do believe the forgiveness came from her Christian beliefs.

Bill
You are very right. True forgiveness has to be associated with one's absolute faith in God. When people truly forgive, they may really mean what they say about forgiveness. Not only do they tend to purge toxicity from their mind, but they also tend to hand over the case of delivering justice to the higher being — God or Nature, as you believe — consciously or otherwise. And, perhaps, they also believe the higher justice is truer and possibly heavier. Dedicated missionaries, like

Staines, work from good faith to uplift the underprivileged from the lowest rungs of the socio-economic ladder. Such people may have no socio-politico-religious motives but to dedicate their lives to serving God's underprivileged people.

Vijay
I wrote on the topic of forgiveness from the point of view of my personal observations and experience. To be truthful, I would not forgive if I was in Mrs Staines's shoes. I do not believe every individual gets what we call God's justice or that it is an ethical universe where everything happens for the best. I think the creative principle, which is not a human-like being in the sky, is an energy and natural intelligence, what you might call the Supreme Being. But once created, humans are on their own and d evil or good, and humans have to cope with it.

If you say God is fully responsible for everything, then He is also responsible for all the misery and cruelty in the world. I say no to that theory. I believe man is responsible for what he does and must cope with it, as Jean-Paul Sartre (a French philosopher, 1905–1980) said: 'Man is condemned to be free.'

When we say God will punish an evil-doer, then we outsource our revenge to God. That is all. The sense of revenge remains. This is an endless question. It is my reading of the Gita that evil must be fought and destroyed. Gandhi read non-violence into the Gita, which I do not agree with. Non-violence is a limited theory; it does not work in many cases.

Bill
These are eternal questions. These questions will always remain. I agree with you about the theory of the Supreme Being. But I believe the greatest revenge and the sole pathway to self-healing is indeed forgiveness. Yes, we tend to outsource our revenge to God, perhaps to free ourselves, unconsciously. I am in full agreement with your God

concept. I still have an element of belief in the theory of Karma, but I am not sure how long this belief will stay with me.

Vijay
We each have to work it out, I guess. Everything in spiritual matters is a belief. We know nothing.

Bill
Yes, we know nothing. And that truth has not changed since the days of Socrates. He always maintained that he knew nothing. Vijay, I have two questions for you:
- Can or cannot forgetting and forgiving go together?
- Is it impossible to forget without forgiving? Or is it the other way round?

Vijay
Yes, I believe that you don't ever forget a hurt but you can still partly forgive. I say partly forgive, since you do believe the holy books and teachings that tell you so. And you want to do so also since you are a civilised and pacifist kind of person. You very effectively put the anger and hurt aside and still are nice and normal with that person or persons. I call that partial forgiveness.

I think the answer to your second question is the same.

As I have been saying, there is neither total forgetting nor total forgiving. I think you just work out a kind of peace inside yourself and that is a wise thing to do.

Impractical idealism

There is a lot of idealism about this matter of forgiveness. And, as someone who believes very realistically that the world is as it is, I am very suspicious of the effectiveness of too much idealism. There are

Chapter 4 FORGIVE AND FORGET

beautiful teachings, for instance in Christianity, about non-violence and forgiveness. The Sermon on the Mount is a most inspiring and beautiful teaching on this. But who really ever 'turns the other cheek'? After Christ, there was so much violence and aggression in Christianity. The Crusaders were the biggest example of organised violence in the name of religion and God. Similarly, Islam, a religion that emerged from conflict, preaches brotherhood and peace. But the followers of these religions and others have been fighting wars for centuries.

So you see why I am very sceptical about idealism. In all traditions, including Hinduism, there is absolutely noble and sublime idealism. But it is never put into practice. The same goes for all this tremendous idealism on forgetting and forgiving.

I do not for a moment dismiss the idealism, Bill. I say this because you are a pacifist and deeply committed humanist. I think it's great to have people like you. It is the idealists and visionaries of humanism who always show the way.

I am someone who believes in the highest and best of humankind, and yet one who sees the ugliness and the lowest that humans do. We must learn from it and accept it. And having done that, having understood that humans are both good and evil, we must deal with it. This is all in the context of your questions about forgiving and forgetting.

Deal with it, the only practical way

I had earlier given you the example of Mrs Staines, whose husband and two sons were killed by a mob. She later said that with her belief in Christ, she forgave the killers. I do not think ordinary people can do this.

That is why I say one has to *deal with it*. As a correspondent and writer, I once did a three-part feature on war widows. I met wives of soldiers who were killed by the soldiers of the Pakistani army. The women I met were mostly in their thirties and forties and had children.

Their lives had been devastated. And yet I saw, to my surprise and sadness at the cruelty of life, that many of these women handled it all bravely. They did not express hate for the Muslims and Pakistanis.

They just kept quiet when I asked them about the 'enemy'. There was one army wife, whose husband had been a colonel, who was very articulate: 'It was a war. It is terrible, of course, terrible for all of us. But our soldiers and their soldiers, they both have to do the same. What else can I say?' I understood something that day. That she and the others had learnt to deal with it. They lived with their loss as they had to. But they also had put some of the hurt aside.

The same experience repeated itself for me soon after the horrible anti-Sikh riots in 1984. There were terrible reports of how mobs killed and burnt and ravaged the Sikhs in many cities of India. It was a bloody, communal persecution and innocent Sikhs were killed all over India. I was a news correspondent at that time in Delhi and saw some very ugly scenes. Nearly 3,000 Sikhs were killed by mobs in the city. It was a terrible phase of violence and cruelty. I was a witness to the power of evil that transforms normal men into demons. Of course, there was anger and bitterness among the Sikhs. That anger and bitterness has never been wiped away from the minds of the women and children who became widows and orphans in the riots. But the Sikhs did not respond with a generalised collective hatred for the Hindus, the main rioters and killers in the mobs. There are Sikhs in every part of India, of course, a large number in the state of Punjab, and they have never attacked or despised and sought revenge from the Hindu community. Here again, they have learnt to deal with it. They have not forgotten. The young Sikh women who became widows in the thousands, and the children who are now adults certainly have the scars. But they neither hate nor burn with revenge. I think this is the best a person or a people can do after such cataclysms of inhumanity.

Majoritarianism — a reaction from the past

Chapter 4 FORGIVE AND FORGET

I brought up the matter of the Sikhs for a reason. I will put it to you here in a moment. As far as I can recall, at least in recent times, the Sikhs, though a martial community, have never been involved in communal riots. I have thought about it. This is in contrast to the Hindus who, though a peaceful and usually non-violent people, have retaliated with equal savagery in communal riots, at least in the last hundred years that I can survey. Especially at the present time, when Hindu majoritarianism is at its peak in India, the Hindus, or at least a section of them, have been extremely aggressive and revengeful.

I think Hindu majoritarian aggression at this point in time is really a reaction of historical revenge against everybody, the Europeans and the Muslims, who has suppressed and dominated them in the past. While Hindu–Muslim riots in India have been commonplace, unfortunately, I do not think there has been Sikh violence of a communal nature for a long time.

In my humble opinion, it all goes back to the religious traditions and ideas of separateness — the 'other' — and an ingrained consciousness of distrust for people of other religions. This could not be said for Hinduism as it has been in the past, for it has been one of the most universal and humanistic religions.

But the long periods of oppression of the Hindus, in fact a very long period of 900 years, have now come out in a new form of revanchism wherein large sections of Hindus believe that they must now be very aggressive and even violent to make up for the weaknesses that were the reason for their oppression.

Added to this is the age-old Hindu tendency, which I call a touch-me-not religious sense of purity and exclusiveness, to regard people from other religions as 'different' and 'other'. Historically, the Hindus have had this feeling that separates them from Muslims and Christians and people of other religions. This is a phenomenon of the last few centuries when the Muslims and the British began to rule India. The Hindus became insular and distrusted all non-Hindus. That is the background from which present-day Hindu aggression and majoritarianism has come about. The Muslims react to this with equal intensity of distrust and so the communal cauldron keeps on the boil. You see, no one forgets.

The Muslims too have a very strong feeling, encouraged of course by their own holy teachings of the *kafir* (or the unbeliever) and the exhortation to jihad. It has been repeatedly pointed out by Muslim scholars that the word is supposed to signify a battle within oneself between good and evil. However, it does not really hold water in the light of events and realities. The sense of distrust of the unbeliever is just too strong. In spite of this, Hindus and Muslims have lived together for centuries and will continue to do so.

The Sikhs belong to a new and very modern religion, which was in fact a kind of reform movement in the fifteenth century against the dogma and ritual and caste differences that had made the Hindus weak. It was a religion of total simplicity. The sanctum sanctorum of the Sikh Gurdwara (temple) holds only a sacred holy book, the Guru Granth Sahib, which has hymns and songs written by people from all castes of the Hindu and Muslim religions. The Sikhs, therefore, have never been taught of otherness or disrespect and dislike for other religions because one of the pillars of the teachings of the Sikh gurus is that of universal brotherhood and humanism.

I think by now, Bill, you would have cottoned on to where I am getting at. It is rather obvious. The older religions of Islam and Hinduism have, by dint of their antiquity and the histories that they have gone through, developed ideas, very strong ideas, of exclusion and superiority. In Sikhism, there is no such thing.

I have gone into this long explanation to take you to an aspect of the subject we are discussing, the human ability to forget and forgive. It is this. While individuals on their own and with their own natures may not go to the extent of violent revenge and have a generalised hatred of another religion, even though people of that religion may have caused harm and hurt, they will still identify with the collective consciousness of wounds that need to be avenged.

I think what I am saying here is that this matter of forgiving and forgetting is also a reflection of family and religious training, even the values of society and the country at a certain time.

As I have put across, some people just deal with it and put it all aside so as to be able to live normal and peaceful lives, even if it is with the people who belong to a group or community that has caused them harm. I would like to discuss this in light of the attitudes of some sections of the Kashmiri Pandits who suffered persecution at the hands of Muslim militants and who now are a very angry people, angry and vengeful. They have reason for being so, but they still have to go back and live with people of the same community.

Anger and revenge are the obvious and immediate reactions when people are made to suffer, whether it is individuals or groups and communities. That is where a certain amount of rationalism, perhaps even some of the noble ideas of idealistic sages, have to be brought into play. I would perhaps describe it best with an oxymoron: what people need is a kind of realistic idealism.

That is my feel on forgiveness. There is one more point I will take up next.

Is forgiveness and acceptance a weakness or cowardice?

Well, Bill, I don't know how a deeply committed pacifist and humanist like you would react to my idea of practical idealism, I would like to see. I think one of the results of modern thinking and questioning is that the lines between rock solid principles and ideas are becoming blurred. We are accepting that different ideas, even opposing ideas, can be partly right.

Ideas of non-violence and peace and even forgiveness, which we are discussing, don't have to be sacrosanct or applicable in all situations.

Forgiveness, kindness and compassion are always noble and take away negativity. But there is an age-old critical challenge here.

It is the charge that forgiveness can also be passivity or a sign of weakness. That it is the easy way out. I think that is not really true. To a large extent, people with great faith in God and in their own sense of values find it possible to forgive. I think Gandhi and his soldiers of non-violence did show us that. So did Martin Luther King in his movement against racialism. I recently came across a passage by Nobel Laureate Toni Morrison in which she said the same thing. The blacks in America today are a new generation with a past of horrible injustices to their ancestors. But they have not been vengeful. They have accepted it was another era in time and their history. 'To forgive', she writes, 'requires extreme strength.'

It is really a matter of what situations prevail at a certain time. Many of the strategies of non-violence Gandhi practised would be of no avail in today's world of aggression and terrorism. It is also very possible that the very cultured, civilised and peace loving become 'too soft' to be able to resist violence. That was partly the story of a highly evolved Indian civilisation in ancient times. India, in the words of historian A. L. Basham (in his book, *The Wonder that Was India*), was the land of plenty, the *soney ki chidiya* (golden bird) which was eyed by conquerors.

A highly evolved and cultured civilisation and its people are liable to shun violence and the barbarity of war. It is an irony of human development. We grow to love peace and positive human values. But we become unable to face violence when attacked.

The answer, if there is one, lies in being able to respond and act as situations demand. We must be noble and idealistic in our human values, but we must not be the victims. There is no better illustration of this than Lord Krishna's exhortation to the warrior Arjuna to fight and destroy evil. But he must do it without anger or hate. The good must fight when necessary to keep the balance of goodness in the world.

I think I have said most of what I have to say on this. Bill, I recall you writing somewhere that it should be possible to feel compassion and sadness for someone, or a group of people, who hurt you once long ago but who are now victims themselves of suffering. Perhaps you could talk about that.

Bill
The examples of the wounded and scarred, physically, mentally and psychologically — the Sikhs and the families of the martyred soldiers — are befitting examples of *dealing with it*, both practically and philosophically.

Our memories are our painful scars; that is what I maintain. I do agree with you on your theory of partial forgiveness.

In the best of cases, the noblest of humans succeed in managing their feelings of vengeance as well as their memories of suffering as victims. It is always partial forgiveness — partial in the sense that they don't carry out any act of retribution against their assailant or an oppressor.

I believe suffering is very important for spiritual growth and growth as a human. But it must churn one to the deepest core. During the *Sagarmanthan*, nectar appeared only after the poison, which Shiva (the *Neelkanth*) drank and held in his throat. If the nectar (forgiveness or partial forgiveness) has not yet appeared, and if poison (vengeance) is still emanating, the person has not suffered enough. Undoubtedly, the person has to suffer much more before nectar comes out.

Have you noticed how the best of gold and diamonds are created? By inflicting significant pain on them! Gold nuggets undergo hell — as imaginatively described in the texts — before pure gold is formed. It is a similar case with diamonds.

I believe it is all a matter of perspective. Our suffering may be our army sergeant at the military academy who trains soldiers hard for their own survival. They hate him during their training, but he turns out to be their saviour during the times of war and hardship. He trains them to survive — to endure mental pain and deal with the physical suffering. Suffering may be our best teacher.

Yes, it is true my emotions metamorphosed quickly as far as my loss of home (Kashmir) in 1989–90 is concerned — from extreme fear and anxiety, a journey through a phase of mental paralysis to helplessness, frustration and anger, which led to my internal reconciliation (dealing with it, as you have described) and finally developed into empathy. I have not been able to understand myself. How can a normal person suffer so much for the same community, in their difficult times, which may have, directly or indirectly, caused his suffering decades ago? But it has happened and I am witnessing it inside me. Perhaps my spirit (system) can't handle any further negative or angry emotions.

Perhaps my internal *Sagarmanthan* has already completed. Whatever the reason, I don't believe in an eye for an eye. As Gandhi said, it would make the whole world blind. The best approach is to deal with it.

It is true we get angry and restless at times — when painful memories surface from the subconscious mind to the conscious mind — but it is also true we experience much more peace and internal stability when we embrace the aggressor.

I fully agree with Toni Morrison that one requires extreme strength to be able to forgive.

Vijay

Yes, Bill, I think you have spoken well on this. That there is suffering and it causes the internal churning which produces something ambrosial out of the poison of anger and bitterness.

The *sagar-manthan* (churning of the oceans) is a mythology that teaches and inspires. It perhaps also shows the way to those who suffer.

What you say about the transformation of pain and suffering into an understanding of life and into a deeper kind of wisdom is very appealing to me. An endless chain of revenge is only self-destructive.

I think there are times when one must 'take up arms against a sea of troubles, and by opposing, end them' (there I go again with Hamlet!). We must fight those who trouble us. And then there are times, especially when much time has passed, when we must move on and live anew.

Bill
Your thoughts are good and concurrent with mine.

Intrinsically, the human spirit endeavours to achieve freedom. To be free and move ahead requires one to break free from past fetters. Our memories of pain are our fetters. Our wishes and desires for miseries to be unleashed — by God or by government — on our adversaries are our fetters. Our fetters imprison us within a vicious web of the past. As such, we miss living the present and future moments of our life; simply, we imprison ourselves.

To be free, we have no other option but to break our fetters. As you have suggested, dealing with it is perhaps the most realistic — practical and philosophical — approach to living free, in a relative sense of course.

Absolute forgiveness can only happen if the sufferer loses all memory of the past, due to dementia or a brain injury. So long as we have memory, absolute forgiveness, such as that professed by idealists as forgiving and forgetting, is impossible and just a speck of dust in the wind.

In conclusion, deal with it if it hurts you. Liberate yourself and move on. Vengeance imprisons you. Break your fetters, which are your thoughts of retribution. Our thoughts and acts of vengeance push our world perpetually from one extreme to another, without an end. As a consequence, we alternate between the states of playing the victim and being seen as the aggressor.

Our lives are lost either in defending ourselves from our aggressors or in taking revenge against our aggressors. In both states, we just live a perpetual hell.

Stay in the middle, stabilise and deal with it, without contemplating any vengeful act against our aggressor, who may have been our victim in the past. The one and the only way we can free ourselves from this perpetual hell is to stabilise ourselves in the middle and not allow ourselves to dangle between the extremes of defence and aggression. It is also true that, in this middle state, many ignorant souls may deem us cowards and our pacifist position as cowardice. I believe the highest bravery lies in non-violence and partial forgiveness, without causing the same or more suffering on our aggressors than they may have earlier caused us. Lord Shiva (as *Neelkanth*) and Jesus Christ have showed us that way.

Forgiveness means freeing yourself and the other person from the anger you have against that person. One should try to rid oneself of anger and be free. Anger is toxic; it clouds our wisdom and natural self. It sickens our body, mind and spirit.

Chapter 5

SCIENCE, RELIGION AND SPIRITUALITY

Science, religion and spirituality — the charmed triangle of our lives

At an international conference on Science, Mathematics and technology education in November 2019, as providence had it Bill interacted closely with Kenneth Tobin, a world-famous science educator who has published over 400 books, chapters and journal articles on the topics of science education, teacher education, emotions, wellness and research methods. Among many other things — about life and death, human emotions and wellness — Ken said he had been taught how to see energy fields around living beings; he learnt it first with plants and then graduated to humans. Bill shared his thoughts with Ken about how plants could be connected with one another. Using a similar analogy, Bill also suggested that humans too could be interconnected.

Bill
In this chapter, we should also discuss the religion of science — called scientism – and how it limits our range of thinking, similar to our belief systems.

Vijay
I can feel the excitement and interest of yours in meeting with Ken Tobin, especially after reading his bio. What a tremendous amount and

range of work! I am so glad you interacted with Tobin and discussed some of the subjects that we are looking at in our book. I will look into this religion or fad, as I call it, of science you term as scientism. There are new systems and new ideas today and that is inevitable, not always good. Every age does and should create new ways. The problem comes in when these new ideas, borne of genuine questioning and free thinking, also become religions. When they take on the authority and exclusiveness of the final word, then they all become dogmatic and narrow and limiting.

Har daur mein naya mazhab, naya khuda paya ...
Every age presented a new god and a new religion ...

Bill
I have previously spoken about the risks of scientism in mental health in my earlier book, *My Life Does Not Have to be Unhappy* (2017). I have been inspired by the thoughts of the Harvard law professor Michael Sandel. Michael is a philosopher and has spoken about scientism and how it is replacing other 'isms' but with similar consequences.

Science is a path that rational humans use to uncover the laws of nature. It manifests into a wide range of applied sciences — engineering, technology, medicine and so on — that deal with the wellness of humans.

Spirituality makes us aware of our spiritual existence, other than our physical existence, and how we are connected with all other beings in the spiritual domain. The common factor in 'science' and 'spirituality' is the human as well as the human mind.

Vijay
That is well said, Bill. But, in spite of the human mind being the common factor, we see that the human mind is everywhere in conflict with itself and with other minds. I say this at the outset of our discussion because science on the one hand and religion (and spirituality) on

the other hand have been considered as opposites to each other for a long time. It is interesting to trace how they became human activities to confront each other.

Very early in humankind's evolution, there was no such bifurcation or difference between science and spirituality. In fact, I can point out that all of the profound work in the sciences of astronomy, medicine, chemistry and physics in ancient India was done by the Hindu Rishis, both men and women, who were spiritually trained and were fully or partially renunciates. It was the same in Europe where, once again, it was the monks and friars in holy orders who were involved in study and scholarship. In both cases, science was the study of natural laws. You have pointed to that already.

All knowledge was science. But as religions became organised and more dogmatic, they hardened their certainties that were rooted in belief and faith, in myth and imaginings that were not open to question. It was in the medieval period that religion became so powerful a dominating force that it would accept neither doubt nor change. Those who questioned religion with a scientific mind were punished for blasphemy. It was at that time right up to the sixteenth century that science and religion became two confronting entities. Christianity and Islam both had strict blasphemy laws (some Islamic countries still do) and science was strangulated.

It is important that we put this on record, as we move on, because, though things have changed and science has come into its own, there is always the possibility that religion will encourage fanaticism and bigotry. This is because religion delivers certainties. People want that. Even fantasies and mythologies will do if they are supposed to be sacred.

But we shall see, as we go along, that it is all changing now. More people are thinking and that is a beginning. New bridges are being built to reunite science and spirituality. I do feel very strongly that our future on this planet now depends on a harmonious working together of both. They are two aspects of the human mind and must add to each other as well as pull the reins on each other.

Bill
It is a little baffling why science and spirituality are seen to be working against each other. The way I look at it, as an engineer (using science) and as a spiritualist (practising meditation for nearly three decades), both topics are human-centric and tend to achieve the much needed unification of humans.

Science is a mechanism of uncovering truth and the laws of Nature, which helps to break down the walls constructed by ignorance and fear, and promoted and prompted by religions and various belief systems, between humans. Similarly, spirituality promotes recognition of the same universal spirit in all life forms, even in soils and rocks that we humans generally consider as inert or lifeless. Both science and spirituality bind humans; both transcend belief systems as well as inter-human and intra-human fear, apprehension and suspicion.

Yes, if spirituality is confused with religion, then the two topics may be seen to face each other as adversaries. But religion is not spirituality. Religion tends to divide if understood and followed in half measure — superficially — which happens in most real cases when humans fail to grasp the essence of religious messages and just follow their face value. But spirituality transcends religion. Spirituality is much higher and beyond the bounds of a religion, any religion.

So it is important that a clear distinction is made between spirituality and religion, otherwise this confrontation will continue and humans will lose as a result of the religious silos within which they may have imprisoned themselves.

Vijay
Bill, I think religions too will change — will have to change. This will happen as new generations, new thinking, will reject the archaic. It is

Chapter 5 SCIENCE, RELIGION AND SPIRITUALITY

already happening in many parts of the world. I say this because, in my view, it is religion in its truest and cleanest sense that actually 'delivers' an access to spirituality to the masses.

As you say, 'religion that is half understood' is the problem. This is because it is controlled by people who misuse it. Yet at the simplest level of intelligence and to the ordinary person who is not intellectually or mentally at ease with spiritual practices, it is religion which is the gateway to some kind of higher thinking.

I submit that the beginning of religion, humankind's awe and wonder and questioning, was also the beginning of science.

Bill
From where I stand, science is one of the shades — pathways — of spirituality. It helps us to realise the truth, just as spirituality does. I maintain science and spirituality go hand in hand. The more we realise and know based on the scientific principles, the more empathy we develop for the world around us and the better humans we become.

Spirituality dispels darkness (untruth) and so does science.

Vijay
Well, you have the logical view. What we must always be afraid of is the human factor, the good and the bad of human nature. It is inescapable. What I am getting at is the arrogance that gets into science, which is the quest for knowledge of humankind in awe and wonder; that same science becomes pride, defiance of Nature and the very heavens. I read now that billions of dollars are to be spent in a science project that promises immortality in the next twenty-five years. Imagine that.

We challenge both life and death in our mad hubris. The same is true of religion and spirituality. Our holy men and gurus call themselves *Bhagwan*, which means God. Even other devotees and spiritual people would be gods themselves or find oneness with god. Very religious people are also invariably seen to be very arrogant people. In their pride of goodness, they judge everyone else. So this is the problem. Science unleashed in our modern world has brought the insidious problem of scientism.

Bill

The way I look at it, spirituality is like an ocean — an ocean without boundaries. It contains all laws of Nature, all truths and all thoughts, including the various religious thoughts. At the heart of this unbound ocean lives the Central Station (in your own words). This Central Station is, however, without form — *niraakaar* (formless) — as described in Hinduism and Sikhism. In its true, unbound form, spirituality dispels all darkness and unifies humanity within itself and with all remaining life.

As various levels of spirituality were uncovered by various great men and women — prophets, thinkers, philosophers, scientists and explorers — various religious thoughts were born, which remained bound within the domains of religions. As a matter of fact, all religions share a common message in regard to the common need for goodness of humans and fear of God (except in Buddhism and Sikhism). Deliberate differences came into being. This is similar to various universities having different names, logos, coats of arms, syllabi, academics and so on. These deliberate differences sell. Most outward differences conceal — as a deliberate strategy — a similar core, which contains the main elements of spirituality. I can explain further.

Let us fill a bucket (of infinite capacity) with pure water, colourless and odourless. Now, let us get a few tinted glass bottles of different shapes and sizes and fill them with pure water. Then let us add different edible additives — colours, spices and essences — to each water bottle in varying ratios and proportions. Voila! We have just created various religions from the same water. In its pure form, water was unbound and rather unattractive, dull and boring, without any particular taste or flavour. But in its contained form within each bottle, it becomes much more attractive when different additives, with different colours and flavours, are added to it to suit different people. People have different tastes and preferences, and they choose their faiths and beliefs according to their needs and perceptions. One mould does not fit all.

Now consider yourself as a leader, scholar, seller, proprietor of a religion. Would you like any changes in the brand you are selling if it is selling well? Obviously, no! Won't you highlight the advantages and trueness of your brand of religion? Yes! Will you like any competition? No! So what does it all mean? It all means making the boundaries of your religion rigid to help it to sustain the challenges from its competitors for its survival. It is a no-brainer that the proponents of religions feel threatened by spirituality — which promotes our unbound existence — as well as by scientific revelations, which demystify and deconstruct baseless, unfounded beliefs, stigmas and fears.

Vijay
Yes, religions at this time are very sorely threatened. Perhaps that is why we see so much fanaticism and fundamentalism now in this Space Age. The religions are fighting back. And, strangely, religions are threatened by our new spirituality. This new spirituality, which I will like to talk about in a moment, is saying you can be spiritual without religion and without God.

Bill
Of course, there will be a reaction to the rigidity and fanaticism propagated by religions. How do you expect thinkers and scientists to accept beliefs which have little or no footing? How do you expect scientists to accept things blindly? They have all discovered oneness in humans, who share 99.9 percent of their DNA.

Scientific findings give rise to the modern-day spirituality which does not really need to stand on any religious footing. The problem is that, in doing so, they have the tendency to miss out on the goodness and the core objectives of religions, that is to make good and moral human beings and instil hope in them.

Vijay
Yes, this is an immense problem: that science concerns itself only with physical phenomena. There is another world of feelings, emotions and ideas that are non-physical. There are dreams, occult and other concerns, the afterlife and the very mystery of life itself. These are things that cannot be studied according to the existing methods of science. Perhaps new methods and instruments will be invented because at some stage science will have to confront those questions.

The other point I would like to make here is that modern science is fuelled by huge amounts of funding. This normally comes from corporations and from the government, which ultimately want to make use of the findings in the form of inventions and new technology that will make money. This also is a limitation to science which prevents it from going into areas that are not potentially profitable.

You see what I am getting at. That in religion as well as in science there has to be an inflow of money and commercialism. That is perhaps necessary. It is up to the people who work in both areas to try to keep a balance and this can only come if those people are motivated enough in their disciplines to be able to pursue the real and intrinsic purposes of their calling.

Prophets and the messiahs

From what I have said, I don't get the impression that I go against religions. I think religions, when they came from the prophets and the messiahs, were the manifestation of humankind's highest thoughts and yearnings. Those yearnings are part of our own evolutionary movement from the gross to the subtle and sublime. We will always be like that.

The religions began in the great innocence and the infancy of

Chapter 5 SCIENCE, RELIGION AND SPIRITUALITY

humankind's intelligence. It was another world in another time. And there lies the rub. The entire world and its civilisations have changed but our oldest religions have not. It does not work. It does not work at all.

And it was inevitable that there would be a degeneration and misuse of religious power and authority by ambitious men. They could be good men and pious men, but they used religious authority to oppress and to demand obedience. In spite of that, I still hold that religions gave us our most beautiful arts and cultures. Our most profound and lofty philosophies too came from religions, all religions.

I have been very close to a great artist of the string musical instrument called the sarod. This artist, Ustad Amjad Ali Khan, and I were young men nearly a half century ago and were starting out in life. I bring this up because Amjad was a talented musician and was keen to compose new ragas (a raga or rag in Indian classical music is a melodic mode or tune for improvisation). He hummed the basic lines and they were a prayer to Lord Krishna. He then went on to talk about how his music would celebrate devotion to Lord Krishna. I was young enough and friendly enough with Amjad to ask him how as a Muslim he was working on devotional music to a Hindu god.

Well informed in traditions of his music, Amjad then spoke at length on how some of the greatest classical musicians of India were Muslims and they played the raga compositions of ancient India, which were all creations of Hindu musicians and were based on Hindu mythologies. So you see, at the levels of artistic and spiritual integrity, religion has been beautiful and universal.

But the beauty and sublime spirituality of religions was marred by their being used as instruments of power and cruelty and oppression. Because of the unchanging dogma and inability of religions to change, men of intelligence, men of questioning minds, began many centuries ago to turn away from the evils that had crept into all the major religions. This trend became more pronounced after World War II when the horrors of war in God's world turned people away from belief in God and religion. The revolt and disenchantment with religion and its gods has become even more pronounced in the new millennium.

It is not all about disbelief and atheism. It is disbelief in religion and its ways. Most people still need a divinity and transcendence centred on a godlike being, a powerful creative intelligence. They need a personal myth of kindness, compassion and hope.

Bill

As noted earlier, for material reasons, religions have come to become sources of wealth accumulation as well as pathways to power. You may realise the leaders of religions — gurus, imams, bishops — have historically lived and functioned very close to the power of kings and king-makers. These religious heads exploited not only the ignorance of the common masses but also that of the king.

They used a carrot and stick policy to help their motives. The religious heads invoked the fear of death, doom and hell if one did not please the gods, as advised by them. They also promised good health, prosperity, power and procreation if one followed them as a good student. Most importantly, they had the following of the poor and ignorant masses that feared death and the afterlife.

As these religious heads cleverly feasted on the general ignorance of people — especially in relation to the threat of going to eternal hell for defaulting and the promise of going to heaven for conformance, as well as the promise of birth of the family heir (usually a male child) and the fear of death — they commanded a large public following, which the king could not ignore.

Vijay

The antipathy to religion has now created a new secular spirituality. Sam Harris and other scientists are writing books on spirituality. There is some justification as science has an element of the mystical. Aldous

Huxley spoke about mysticism in science decades ago. Scientists like Stephen Hawking, Michio Kaku and others have also pondered about God and Divinity. Dr Kaku, a theoretical physicist and founder of the string theory of the universe, made a bit of a splash a few years ago when he announced that the order and design of the cosmos showed there was a 'designer' or a 'god'.

There is a dialogue between scientists and spiritual leaders like the Dalai Lama. But traditional religious leaders are shut out of this need for a new and more relevant, all inclusive, belief system.

I often tell the story of my literary mentor, the late Khushwant Singh, an iconic writer and editor of India. He said he was an agnostic but went to *gurudwaras* when depressed, translated Guru Nanak's holy verses, and remained a Sikh in dress and culture. He denied the limitations of his religion and was interested in all faiths. There was a certain kind of free thinking and criss-crossing of personal beliefs.

Take the case of Sartre. After a lifetime of atheistic existentialism, on his deathbed Sartre recanted and said, 'Someone was responsible to create me. I cannot believe I was just a speck of dust.'

I think the truth really is that mainstream positions are always suspect and are always limiting. In this age of science, there are dangers of the hegemony of science replacing the hegemony of religion — scientism.

The neurosurgeons and cell biologists writing on spirituality today are not the final word either and science must not arrogate to itself the claim for final truth. Perhaps there is no final truth but there are many truths. Indian Upanishads accept this. Original Vedic Hinduism accepts it too: *Ekam sat, vipra bahuda vadanti* (There is one truth spoken in many ways by the wise). Jiddu Krishnamurti rejected being a world teacher and said truth is a pathless land.

Religions will change slowly but surely. The new age of science will force people to think and evaluate old dogma. To illustrate this, we have the example of how Buddhism changed as it travelled. Finally, it became Zen.

Religion will shed the gross and become personal; perhaps more subtle. The balance of science and mystical spirituality is already there and will increase.

The great discoveries of Bohr, Einstein and Ramanujan in science were made after mystical visions and dreams. Nothing must impinge on our endeavour to seek our freedom through the paths of science and universal spirituality.

Our mission in life should not be merely to survive, but to thrive, and to do so with some passion, some compassion and some humour while trying to live to the fullest. We have been given this life to live and not to be living dead.

Bill

As you said, religions have indeed played their role in shaping the human life and made it colourful and beautiful. Just because, for commercial and competitive reasons, some aspects of religions have been made too rigid and fanatical does not mean religions have lost their validity. Religions still continue to teach us moral values — through epics and stories of virtue and bravery.

Some science students, due to their limited knowledge of both science and spirituality, develop the tendency of turning into atheists. Once that happens, some adopt the new religion of scientism, which is again limited to the bounds of the relative know-how of the individual.

How many students and masters of science can claim to know and understand *all* current scientific knowledge — in all perceivable or imaginable fields of science? None! So scientism is as limited and perhaps dangerous, and divisive, as some of the ignorance and the rigidity of belief systems. It is just like replacing one 'ism' with another 'ism'.

We must agree that science is only a pathway to uncover what is covered. The pathway is unrolling, unfolding with every minute, hour, day, week, month and year. What is known now was unknown in the past. Similarly, what is unknown now may possibly by known tomorrow or the day after.

The human endeavour is constantly trying to know the truth, as is spirituality.

The issue arises mainly due to imparting rigidity to science, spirituality and religion. It is rigidity and exclusivity that is causing discontent and confusion.

Vijay
There are theories and assumptions in both religion and spirituality as well as in science. The difference is, of course, that the assumptions of religion do not ever change and become dogma. The assumptions of science keep changing according to new discoveries and I think that is where science will continue to have more relevance to us. That, of course, is a given.

Yet there is something in common as far as this rigidity in attitudes is concerned. Science too is extremely rigid and emphatic about rejecting all that is non-scientific in religious and spiritual traditions. I think we have to be very careful here because, as we have seen, there is quite a lot in the ideas of religions and spirituality which, though not provable or factual, are still useful to us in understanding the world we live in.

As I have been saying, the total rejection of religion is not wise. And neither is the total dependence on only scientific methods. I find that in the new thinking in spiritual matters today, there is of course a sense of discovery in new directions. But once again, there are not, perhaps cannot be, final truths.

There are good ideas, for instance, such as spirituality without religion or God (though we have had Buddhism as a tradition that has no god). But the atheist scientist who rejects outright all that is in the realm of intuition and pure thought is also being unnecessarily stubborn.

As you have mentioned, we have scientists, neurosurgeons, cell biologists and physicists now talking about spirituality and I think it is a very good trend. What is not good is that they think their way is the only way to go. You see what I am getting at. The scientists are making the same mistake that was made by the people in the religions. They thought they were infallible. Nobody is. And I do not think there is such a thing as an idea or a concept, however wonderful it might be, that will not change with time and with the new needs of a new world.

Let me put it this way. There will always be the spirit of discovery and we will go on bringing other disciplines into trying to understand things around us, questions that we ask from generation to generation. It is being done now. Once again, science has come into the field of spirituality. We are now talking about things like the 'mysticism of science' because it is a reality that some very great scientific discoveries have been made by scientists when they were in a state of dreaming or of trance. I remember a few. The famous physicist Niels Bohr (1885–1962) said that he had developed the model of the atom based on a dream in which he was sitting on the sun with all the planets hissing around. Einstein often said that his entire career was an extended meditation on a dream he had as a teenager. He dreamt that he was riding a sled down a steep snowy slope and, as he approached the speed of light in his dream, the colours all blended into one. He spent much of his career inspired by his dream, thinking about what happens at the speed of light.

And, of course, I cannot forget the work of the Indian mathematical genius Srinivas Ramanujan (1887–1920), who has given the world hundreds of mathematical theorems and questions which are still being studied by modern mathematicians. Ramanujan had famously said, 'My mathematical equations are worthless if they do not reveal an aspect of God.' He had told his colleagues how he got his equations, which he credited to his goddess in South India. Ramanujan said that he got dreams in which he saw mathematical equations written on a blood-red surface.

Bill

For that matter, the German organic chemist Friedrich August Kekulé (Friedrich August Kekule von Stradonitz, 1829–1896), who is acknowledged as the principal founder of the theory of chemical structure, is famous for his work on the structure of benzene. In 1865 he published a paper suggesting that the structure contained a six-membered ring of carbon atoms with alternating single and double bonds. He said that he had discovered the ring shape of the benzene molecule in a reverie or day dream wherein he saw a snake seizing its own tail.

Vijay

The point of all this is that just as religion must change and evolve to accept new ideas and new thinking, so must science also begin to look at and investigate the claims of all spiritualists and to find out more about spiritual experiences, such as states of trance and states of epiphany. And we shall doubtless have a spirituality that will be of value in our lives when both work in harmony.

There are no final or unchangeable truths. New ideas and new discoveries will come to humankind in every age and, as we know, every age is changed by its technologies and discoveries. Humankind has different needs and different challenges at different times. I think what we should be looking for in science as well as religion and spirituality is the information and the ideas that will help us. We cannot and must not lose the wonder and the mystery that keeps us thinking. Ultimately, both science and spirituality must help us live better lives as better humans. Nothing must dominate our freedom.

Bill

I do agree with Khushwant Singh's claim of being 'agnostic'. In doing so, he kept his mind and vision open to anything and everyone. He did not outright reject or preclude anything. 'I don't know' has the Socratic wisdom in it. After all, how much do we really know? As Isaac Newton said, 'If you claim God does not exist, you have not understood enough.'

Vijay

I think in their own ways, the people who call themselves agnostics or freethinkers really do manage to get the best of both worlds as they are completely open to whatever appeals to their mind and their own independent worldview. I have met many such men and women who believe in what they want to believe and who give a wide berth to any kind compartmentalisation of their identity. You cannot call them this or that.

Such people, to my mind, have really understood the whole business of making choices or, actually, of not making choices. They refuse to be labelled. On a personal note, I can empathise with them quite easily. This is because when there is complete freedom of mind at once, one can at least try to get away from most of the conditioning; there are no boundaries.

There is a thought I have on this matter of boundaries. Every human system or organisation which begins with a good idea and tries to do good for people and for society in time adds a lot of baggage of organising – for example, managing people, administration, decision-making, keeping reputations intact – which I really feel is 'over-organisation', and it becomes a heavy and unmanageable, also an unfriendly, kind of system. Well, I suppose that is how it is and will not change and perhaps that is why a greater amount of individualism is, therefore, necessary in making the right balance to live intelligently.

I think the real fun of it all is, in the fact that you understand, whether it is science or whether it is spirituality, you can take what you want and in any form you want, as far as it suits your own thinking and needs.

I have already mentioned the writer Khushwant Singh, who called himself variously an agnostic and sometimes an atheist. As he once joked: 'It also helps sell my books.' But though he rejected religions, he remained a Sikh and took from Sikhism what he needed.

Chapter 5 SCIENCE, RELIGION AND SPIRITUALITY

He was also a great scholar of all the major religions and quoted often from all of them. In fact, Khushwant ruffled a few feathers when he said that there was much in the philosophy of Sikhism that was based on the Hindu Upanishads. He was right, of course, and scholars after him have accepted this.

Another example I would like to tell you about is of the writer Nirad Chaudhary. He was someone I met often for interviews as he loved to talk to the press. He famously said: 'Religion is a revolt against death.' What he was saying here was that all religions promise people an afterlife and immortality and he did not believe in it. Yet he was a great student of the Vedanta philosophy and wrote reams on Hinduism and how it had changed.

Science is discovery and knowledge and is invaluable as an activity of humans. Yet it does not address something that is of the greatest importance in the life of human beings. Fear! I thought of this as I recall a line from T. S. Eliot: *Come to me, and I shall show you fear in a handful of dust*. There is fear, a primal fear of life and what it can do to us, of death and what will happen to us. Fear of the unknown.

Religion and beliefs and even the myths that humans have created address this fear. The mythologies of religion are stories that a civilisation tells itself and even though it is fantasy, it helps people to get over their fear, to give them hope.

Bill

As the unbound can't be contained in a bound vessel, religion too is not capable of containing the Infinite and unbound spirituality. The same goes with science, which is limited in terms of offering any evidence which it has not yet found as well as evolving with each moment.

Having an open mind to understand, recognise and then negotiate the absurdity in the rigid and bound, human-made concepts of God and spirituality is perhaps the way to go, without harnessing and promoting any reductive, conclusive or narrow tendencies in the practices — thoughts and actions — of any religion. Inclusiveness is the only way forwards in order to sustain a peaceful coherence of humans on Earth.

The above conversation ended with the following humour.

Vijay

Wow! A pollution mask has been put on *Shiva Lingam* (the stone phallic symbol of Lord Shiva) in Varanasi to protect God from foul air! We are a great people indeed. I laughed this morning on reading that people in Varanasi had put pollution masks on a *Shiva Lingham* and on the faces of other gods and goddesses as well. The point is, you can't really blame them because though it was and looked funny, the pollution levels have been extremely high due to the winter haze and overcast weather.

But I also recalled something written by American philosopher Joseph Campbell. He once said in India the people do of course worship God, as all do. But he emphasised that, 'in India they experience God on a one to one basis. God is there as friend and companion.'

And I thought this pollution mask for gods proves Campbell right. The gods are real and there with their devotees as friends, as loved ones.

Bill

It is a very clever gesture — as by a court jester — by those who did it. I think these people are trying to convey to the world that, in India, even God is suffering from air pollution and needs to be protected. That may also be hinting that air pollution in India is beyond even God's control. Indirectly, it may also mean that God needs human endeavour to help Its Creation.

I think this interesting and incoherent triangle formed by religion, spirituality and science is our main area of focus. This triangle directly and indirectly affects all life on the planet — humans and all other life forms. Each apex has been, and is being, misused and abused by the humans wielding power and influence, which comprises less than 1 percent of humankind. The remaining 99 percent of humans struggle to survive but are unfortunately used, abused and exploited by that minuscule minority. Even science is used to exploit people through the tweaking of scientific facts, as religion and spirituality are tweaked, but only for materialistic motives.

I come across many well-educated people who say religion is the main problem plaguing the earth. As such, they support the idea of banning all religions, albeit hypothetically if it was at all possible. When you engage with such individuals in more depth, one gets an uncomfortable feeling that they too may be tending towards an extreme, intolerant front, which I call the 'third front'. The problem is, in doing so — knowingly or unknowingly, deliberately or inadvertently — such people, who are otherwise socially responsible, noble and well meaning, may be promoting an 'anti-religion' thought — a thought that may be based mostly on scientism, which is ever evolving, a thought that appears dangerously to be as rigid or potentially as aggressive as any other extreme thought of any other religion.

Banning religions or having 'no religion' is not a solution to current or foreseeable or potential world problems. Developing tolerance and respect towards humans in all religions is a more prudent and peaceful path to follow. One should be free to follow any religious faith, which one may adopt or may have been born into, but at the same time one should also be free not to follow any religious faith at all and still accepted by religious people and deemed respectable despite being irreligious. Importantly, the focus must be on upholding the intrinsic human dignity of men and women of all religions; developing mutual respect with everyone without stereotyping people; being humane towards one and all; living and working coherently to serve humanity in general; and, most importantly, proactively saving the planet in the process — its ecosystem, environment and all life forms.

During my morning runs, I see an old woman who can barely walk due to her age but still carries her old pet dog in her lap during her short, snail-paced morning walks. Carrying a few extra kilos must logically be making her physical movement more difficult, but her love for her pet transcends her personal pain. Humans can amazingly forget their personal discomforts in living their unconditional humaneness. Mutual empathy and care keep the world going and render it sustainable. To me, humanism is the greatest religion of all and service to humanity is the greatest service one can possibly offer. It is time for us to think and contemplate and ask ourselves a few questions: why I am here? What is the difference between that worm on the ground and me? How do I help to bring peace and progress in this world?

To conclude, religion and spirituality are two different things. With time, religion may become practically redundant. It thrives on the general ignorance and superstition of the masses, which science upturns. Religion is generally based on beliefs, which can be challenged. Spirituality does not need religion but religion needs spirituality. Science promotes spirituality, both are inclusive. Both dispel fear and ignorance, the two ingredients that religion thrives on. The greatest threat to religion is from its own rigidity. To survive, it will have to adapt to the changing times, be more inclusive and dump the aspects that don't withstand the scrutiny of science. Belief without rationalism will not be able to render religion credibility and infallibility.

If religion does not make you a good human, what is it for? If science, technology and education are not used for the general welfare of humanity, what are they for? If spirituality does not bring peace within you and radiate peace to the world around you, what is it for?

Chapter 6

THE TRUTH AND NOTHING BUT THE TRUTH

The Truth obsession closes our minds to natural living

The search for something called the Truth has been an obsessive quest for humankind from the earliest times. It has led us to the knowledge, science and wisdom we have today. That is the positive aspect. But when the concept of Truth is amorphous and extremely idealistic, it has also led to didacticism and aggressive supremacies.

Pontius Pilate questioned Jesus as to his claim that he was 'witness to the truth'. 'What is truth?' asked Pilate (*Quid est veritas?* John 18:37–38). He did not stay for an answer. Pilate was the fifth governor of the Roman province of Judaea and known to have presided over the trial of Jesus and ordered his crucifixion. Following this question, he had proclaimed to the masses ('the Jews') that he did not consider Jesus guilty of any crime. As per the Gospels, Pilate was reluctant to execute Jesus. He is believed to have converted to Christianity and is venerated as a martyr and saint.

Vijay
That's one of the oldest questions in the world. It has been answered, or shall I say, sought to be answered, in myriad ways — by wise men, religious people, spiritual thinkers and, of course, by scientists and

philosophers. Personally, I can never forget the words of spiritual master Jiddu Krishnamurti, who said, 'Truth is a pathless land.' Quite simply, we all find our own paths.

Bill
When we talk about Truth, are we talking about the Truth or infinite realities or why things happen as they happen — the physical laws — and for what purpose? In short, is the Truth — One Truth —what this is all about and why?

By the Truth, I mean One Truth — One Certainty — One Absolute Certainty — One Common Certainty — One Eternal Certainty.

From Jiddu Krishnamurti's assertion that 'Truth is a pathless land', I infer perhaps he meant all those infinite realities, in all those infinite directions, in those ten dimensions (*Dus Dishayen*) — which is understood and defined now as the multiverse — those infinite number of individual little truths that radiate from the One Truth that may be the reason or the cause of all that we call life or the cosmos or the universe.

And Jiddu sounded so right. In a two-dimensional system, we have 360 degrees around a point. A circle is a two-dimensional figure. But imagine the intricacy when we talk about a spherical object and try to imagine the directions of rays emanating from the core of that sphere. Is it possible to even imagine the number of those directions? Now consider a multiverse. Even mathematically, certain things are considered 'indeterminate'. In such a case, 'the truth' (in lower case) is indeed a pathless land.

In so far as the Truth — One Common Truth — is concerned, I see that as One Intelligent Mind that uses an Intelligent Hand to turn on and off the Main Switch at the Power Station that supplies electric power along all power transmission lines, grid stations, power transformers and power appliances. That One Intelligent Mind is the Truth. (We may even use the analogy of the sun in our solar system. But in the Milky Way, there are many suns. How many suns do we talk about?)

Chapter 6 THE TRUTH AND NOTHING BUT THE TRUTH

Well, we may be able to uncover the truths — laws and realities — that run those electric appliances, grid stations, power lines, the Power Station and the Main Switch, but how do we understand the working of the Intelligent Hand? Even if we are able to reach there, how do we understand the Intelligent Mind that uses the Intelligent Hand to operate the Main Switch? (In the same way, how do we know exactly when and how the cosmos was created and, most importantly, by whom? Was it all random?)

At a gross level, as a most simplified thought, the One Certainty — the Truth — seems to be the 'death' of everything, every being, that is created. Death is the only certainty, other than the movements of the planets. But *who* has created 'death' and the movement of those planets as well as the sun, the Milky Way and black holes, and *why*? The human mind has been trying to figure this out. And the pursuit of knowing this truth will keep us humans engaged perhaps for as long as our race exists.

Do you know neuroscience knows only less than 10 percent about how the human brain works? The first decade of this millennium was dedicated to the study of the brain.

Vijay
Yes, there has been in recent times a great amount of activity by neuroscientists, apart from scientists in other fields, in the area of spirituality. We do know of the great success in spirituality of neuroscientist Sam Harris with his books and lectures, as noted in Chapter 2. An Indian neuroscientist in the USA named Abhijit Naskar has also created a spiritual following with his books, gathered into a collection titled *Neuro Sutra*, obviously named after the ancient Indian text *The Brahma Sutra*.

Bill, all this is new and exciting but I have a reading on this. It is that what is happening is another era and generation finding new paths and new ways. Every age does that. These new paths and new ways fulfil current and new needs.

I think the Great Mystery, the Truth, if you prefer to call it so, will always remain. And that is necessary for humankind.

Bill

You are absolutely correct. Without our unending engagement in unlocking the mystery of the Truth, we may possibly become directionless, purposeless, aimless and, perhaps, lifeless. Our inquisitive nature keeps us going, interested and engaged.

The Great Mystery — the Intelligent Mind — will always keep our soul restless and mind working. Verily, we may seem to be slowly making progress to know the Infinite Truth but we may possibly never reach there. Can a finite mind ever be able to contain an infinite reality? Our imagination feeds our pursuit of knowing and vice versa. Can we ever know something which is even beyond our wildest imagination?

Somehow, I believe when neuroscience fully unlocks the mystery of the human brain — that is, when we fully know how it really works — that will be the moment we may know the Truth — the One Truth. It is possible we may have carried the Truth with us all along, in all ages, without having unlocked it from within our own heads. All along, since we started thinking and contemplating, we may have looked for it mainly outwards and upwards but not really tried to seek it within us. So it has remained elusive.

Truth has to be within us only as we personify the entire universe. That is my belief. Isn't the cause of human design or, for that matter, life itself, a mystery?

Vijay

Like some other eternal questions that have kept us company through the centuries, this Truth quest is endless. I think it is also important that we have such questions. Questions that make us think and explore but which are never fully answered.

Before I forget, however, let me share a true story that is both amusing and apocryphal. I think you'll like it given the context in which we are speaking. A writer friend visited a young godman in India for an interview. The godman had a large spiritual corporation running well with branches and devotees all over the world. He was a young man who had just ascended the so-called spiritual *gaddi* (seat, throne) after the demise of his father.

During the interview, the godman gave confident answers. One of the questions that came up was why or for what reason did so many thousands of people come to him in their spiritual quest. The godman directed the question smilingly to a foreigner, a devotee from America. 'I have come to the guru after years of seeking the answers to my inner questions. I have been searching for the Truth and I found it here,' the American said.

The godman took up the cue. 'You see,' he said, matter of factly, 'all my devotees will tell you this. I have the Truth. My father had it and gave it to me. The Truth of life and God and this illusory world. You might say that I keep the Truth in my bank. Now when a devotee comes to me for the Truth, he or she has to get a cheque signed by me to get the Truth out of the bank.'

Bill
It may look strange to some of us but the fact is many, or rather most, of us believe there is a key to Truth which remains in the custody of some special people. People don't realise that we humans are all alike — with the same faculties, with 99.9 percent of the same DNA, the same weaknesses and, most importantly, all being mortal. We are all subject to sickness, disease and death. If that is the case, how can only some of us have the keys to the Truth? It is this general ignorance in most of us which some of us, the self-proclaimed gurus and godmen, cash in on. Are we not all godmen, godwomen or godchildren?

On a lighter note, during my college days, there used to be a custom-tailor shop in Mohan Singh Place building, at Connaught Circus in

Delhi, called Godson. Every year, during my winter holidays, I used to get half a dozen denim, canvas and corduroy jeans stitched there. On the back right pocket the jeans would carry a leather label: Godson. This was a time when most jeans would carry popular brand labels, like Levi's and Wrangler. My friends and peers would be intrigued by my Godson label. But wasn't that so apt? Should we not all carry that label, Godson, or Godchildren?

These commercial gurus and godmen have always intrigued me. If they were truly realised, they would be living 'normal' lives. But they don't. They tend to enjoy all the material wealth that one can imagine exists in the world, including the much needed attention from media, politicians and the general public. How bloated they look when people prostrate before them! Human ignorance has always been exploited by the cleverer individuals among us, the more conniving ones.

These godmen — usually under the protection of their bodyguards, surrounded by their sidekicks and henchmen, and with the blessings of clever politicians — have the gift of the gab. They are usually great actors. They use fear as their main weapon to exploit mass ignorance. In so many ways, they actually act as middlemen, or brokers, or even as agents for politicians who use them as political influencers of the masses. All you need to do is grow a long, white beard and wear an unusual outfit, usually a retro gown with retro headgear.

Any educated person, with a little bit of intelligence, people skills and knowledge about human psychology, political science, world history, religion, geography and the epics can project himself or herself as a godman (*guru*) or a godwoman (*guru-mata*). Plus, if you can speak fluent English, your success as a career guru is assured; you will travel the world many times over, speak to professional audiences, be widely interviewed as a socio-political influencer, and find yourself in the inner circle of powerful politicians.

Vijay

Yes, of course, there are always extremely serious and pious protestations from these people who seem to assert that they know everything. It is even more amusing that millions of people believe them. But that is how it has been for a long, long time. The reason, of course, is that people want their gods and their spirituality like fast food. They want to gobble up everything or be gobbled up without going through the torture of thinking, questioning and being riddled with doubt.

I do think also that we have, for a long, long time, separated our own lives in the world from how we must live and what we think is spirituality. I think I have said this before. We create great ideals, for instance the Truth, and run after them and do all sorts of things to tell ourselves that we are living at a higher level. But we do not look after the smallest and the most mundane things in life that really matter. The world would be a better place if we gave more attention to just living well as good humans.

In the materialistic world and physical sciences, our quest for the Truth has led to great inventions and progress. Because in the world of reality as we know it, truth is defined as something concrete: what things really are and how they work, what laws govern them. It is a quest for facts and observable data that can be studied and proved by rational thought. So, the Truth here means very clear understanding of real things. Perhaps, Bill, as a person trained as an engineer, you might go further with this.

Bill

Yes, by scientific inventions and discoveries, humans are uncovering layers of mysteries surrounding how things work. Swami Vivekananda suggested a professor of science is as worthy of respect as a scholar of religion or spirituality. That is Vedanta. After all, isn't it all about knowing the Truth, which we do undoubtedly by unlocking mysteries surrounding those numerous smaller truths. Little by little, scientists are helping us to see what we could not see in the past, helping us to know what we did not know in the past, such as the truth of gravity, the finite life of our sun, the presence of those numerous planets on and outside the furthest boundaries of our solar system, and black holes. We have learnt how to fly in the sky, live high in the sky in those skyscrapers, travel under and over water, communicate across the globe in real time, salvage and use body parts to save lives, and defeat diseases. Verily, we are in the process of knowing ourselves, our infinite human capability as well as our limitations.

Despite our immense scientific progress, we have learnt that we are not much different than other animals cohabiting with us on this planet and, most importantly, we are not infallible or immortal. Whether we realise those numerous little truths — though science or spirituality — we are undoubtedly making progress in our pursuit of the Truth. I believe the day we are able to fully understand the workings of the human brain, we would know the Intelligent Mind using the Intelligent Hand, which manages the Main Switch at that Power Station.

The Truth can be realised only through our observation of Creation right before our eyes and learning lessons from its workings. Every bit of Creation is true in its own right, just like the nose of an elephant or a small piece among a million pieces of a mosaic.

The Truth is the acceptance and inclusion of everything. We are living in the Truth and the Truth is living with us. Within and without, it is all Truth.

There is no place where the Truth does not exist, it is all pervading. To see the Truth, we need to see with much more than our eyes or ears or other senses and then let go, dissolve ourselves in the Truth — total immersion.

Vijay
I think this entire matter of Truth becomes fraught with conflict when it comes into religion. In other contexts of life, obviously, there is a need

for being truthful. It is in human cultures and religion that the Truth is a contentious obsession and an instrument of power and intolerance.

That big, idealistic and dogmatic idea of Truth comes from the same extreme of divine idealism that has inspired humans to create their gods. So, once again, there is a Christian Truth and a Muslim Truth and Hindu Truth and so on. All of them cannot be the Truth — the One Truth — that we have decided is necessary.

One God and One Truth is supposedly a given in metaphysics and religious belief. I need hardly go into the historical evidence that this insistence on One has been the cause, and still is, of conflict and terrorism and wars. The most religious and the good are like the furies of hell when they want to be cruel and inhuman to the Other. What I am leading to, as you have doubtless guessed, is that we must accept and understand the reality of *many truths*. We live in this world with multiple truths in our lives and our cultures and moralities. Only the very silly chauvinist will insist that only his culture and life is true and good, or the best. There is always a conflict in that. And the irony is that this kind of supremacism has caused untold suffering and hate even though it is childish, puerile and silly. Great conquerors and millions of men, entire nations, have gone to war and committed atrocities based on the idea that only their culture, worldview and ways of life are true and good.

There is a dark irony here. All that cruelty is caused by the obsession with the childish idea that 'I am the best, my culture and my country is the best'. Differences in culture and religious belief have caused conflict in our histories. But it is one of the basic ideas of modernism in our time to accept different cultures. Just as we have learned to accept and to live alongside different races and skin colours among humans, it may not always be well practised but full acceptance and equality of all is a basic modern idea.

There is Truth and the same human quality in all. There is also Truth in different beliefs. We accept this in our internationalism. As I said before, not always practising it and not accepting it is the revolt of the regressive.

The Truth — metaphysical, moral or social — changes with time

That revolt, that aggression of tradition and old ideas, is also a part of the modern world. Denial of change and new ideas is a human trait that we seem to have had in every age. For the same old reason, every opposition to change is based on the stubborn defence of an accepted Truth in that time. Once something is believed to be true, humans will kill and be cruel to defend it. Yet, as we know, beliefs change. Even religions change in the wake of reform movements and opposition to dogma that is irrelevant and denied in later ages. Even the gods change. The gods of the Vedic period in Hinduism are not there anymore. Lord Ram and Lord Krishna came much later in what is now called Hinduism. The gods of the other ancient peoples have disappeared. I think we shall talk about this in another segment.

The important point is that the gods who were once the Truth have gone. The Truth too changes. Cultures and moralities that were true once have changed everywhere. Yet humans are never more certain of their belief in their Truth and their good customs of body and mind as when they are confronted with change, reform and new ideas.

Before I go from this train of thought, let me also point out that we only know that the gods of humankind are only a few thousand years old. I am informed by anthropologists and scholars that the personal, human-form gods, or the anthropomorphic gods, only appeared in human civilisations about 4,000 years ago. Humans in the present form have been on this planet for about 200,000 to 300,000 years. What indeed was the Truth and what were the gods, what forms and what beliefs did our oldest ancestors live with? One can only wonder. But one can certainly conclude that humans have lived with different truths.

Chapter 6 THE TRUTH AND NOTHING BUT THE TRUTH

One Truth and One God?

Let us pause a moment to also look at this great Truth that seems to be common to all religions that there is *one* Truth and *one* God. Though Hinduism has thousands of gods and goddesses, even there the original belief is that there is but one Supreme Being called Brahma, who is without form. But the moment one says this, the next moment the proposition collapses because every religion has its own Truth and its own God. So where does one find the one universal Truth? Perhaps it is not there.

Perhaps there are many truths and they are all true. If that sounds full of contradictions, give it another thought. We are conditioned to believe in the oneness of Divinity and Truth. It is quite logical, of course. If something is supposed to be supreme it has to be one, because there cannot be two supreme things. That logic applies also to the concept of God. It is the way in which we think. I recall that for all his life, Stephen Hawking envisioned something that he called the 'theory of everything'. He thought that all the secrets of the universe could be set out in one single theory that would fit into the laws of physics. Of course, it never happened. The theory of everything was a dream.

Scientists who have come after him and those in a field of quantum physics have indeed made great strides in understanding the nature of reality and the nature of what is the Truth behind reality. But always the questions remain. The mystery is always unsolved.

The Truth and reality can be relative

It would be interesting to you when I say that, in fact, what researchers have found today in quantum physics about the illusory nature of reality — that the experiencer of it is vital to the existence of reality — was something that was postulated in the ideas of the second century CE by the Buddhist monk Nagarjuna, who spoke of his theory of *Sunnyata* (emptiness) in which everything that is in existence is dependent on everything else for its existence. For one thing to be real, another and another have to adjust. Nagarjuna went further with this to expound the Two Truths theory, saying that everything that exists has an absolute and a relative existence. The Truth of one is dependent upon the Truth of another. We see from this that Truth and reality can also be relative.

I will come now to the concept of multiple truths, which is interesting and an exciting possibility. Consider for a moment that we know of the existence of a multi-dimensional universe, with many suns and many galaxies, such as a multiverse all around us. Perhaps also other life forms and other species of beings that are not like us humans at all. Or perhaps they are humanlike and similar to us. These beings have totally different minds and totally different structures of consciousness. They are self-fulfilled and self-sufficient unto themselves.

How can we be so absolutely sure that One Intelligence or One Creative Energy is responsible for this multiverse, or that there is One Truth in all the galaxies? This may sound like fantasy but it is not really so obscure when one considers, as we have already said in this discussion, that we all live with different truths and different realities.

Well, these questions are interesting, not because they will provide any answers but because they will provoke us all to think and, more than that, they will tell us that we do not know it all, that this entire business of Truth is a yearning and a desire to know.

To that extent the questions are important to human life but nobody, not in the world of science, and not in the world of religion or spirituality, nobody knows the One Truth and, perhaps, nobody has in the past or ever will.

We will all live, as you have said, with our past experience, knowledge and information, and get closer to the Truth, our Truth, that we find for ourselves.

Chapter 6 THE TRUTH AND NOTHING BUT THE TRUTH

Bill

Like you, I also believe (note the word is 'believe', not 'know') there are many — perhaps millions or many more — little truths like the small individual units of a mosaic of universal dimension. But I find it rather inconceivable that all these millions of individual truths don't emanate or converge into One Truth.

For example, let us talk about the Big Bang. From one single point, a particle, just imagine what has been created: the whole cosmos. *If* the 'theory' of the Big Bang is correct, then everything — every law, every theory, every intelligence, every thought — was embedded within that one single point and came from there.

Now, let us take a look at the theory of the multiverse. For a multiverse system, there must be proper coordination between one dimension and the other. All dimensions must be in coherence and balance to be sustainable. If the dimensions are not interconnected and mutually sustainable, their coexistence is questionable. All dimensions must function individually but still remain interconnected and in equilibrium. It is like the various biological systems in a human body. We have a skeletal system, a nervous system, a cardiovascular system, a circulatory system, a digestive system, endocrinal system and so on. All systems coexist and are born simultaneously when a human is created out of a microscopic sperm crashing into a microscopic ovum.

What I am coming to is, despite infinite truths — some perhaps ever changing, there must be One Truth that keeps it all stable and in balance, otherwise planets will crash into each other or into the sun due to the sun's mass and gravity. Given that we 'believe' there was chaos[11] in the beginning, it must have started from a point, created perhaps by the Big Bang or even before that — from nothing.

---

11 Clara Moskowitz (2010), 'After Big Bang Came Moment of Pure Chaos, Study Finds', https://www.space.com/9255-big-bang-moment-pure-chaos-study-finds.html#:~:text=The%20universe%20was%20in%20chaos,can%20cause%20large%2Dscale%20effects., retrieved on 27 July 2020.

Vijay

I like your mosaic painting analogy. As an idea, perhaps you would like to go into the thought that if the individual is intelligent and fully aware, he or she can create their own mosaic painting. It is a lonely business but the spiritually aware and the wise most often create their own belief system in worldly life as well as in their spiritual ways of dealing with the eternal questions.

Bill

Yes, fully agreed. Our individual minds are instruments; they work differently in different people. They create their own realities and images of the Truth.

Multiple truths

Vijay

We have introduced a new element of multiple truths. It is a bit bold but I think there is a point to it. If there are other worlds and galaxies, how do we presume there is One Intelligence alone? The idea of One Intelligence probably originates in the idea of One God or One Supreme Being. We think as humans and think of a Being, usually a humanoid. But it is a *formless* Intelligence, an Energy, without any definite form, and not like a human. If there are different worlds and galaxies, there can be self-sufficient intelligences and creative laws.

This is not even atheism — the creative intelligence in Nature and the cosmos is the Supreme Power. You may believe in a god or you may not. As long as you know that you exist, all other things and phenomena exist because of an inner creative energy.

All comes from Nothingness

Chapter 6 THE TRUTH AND NOTHING BUT THE TRUTH

Let me tell you about the concept of Nothingness. The seed of anything and all matter is the atom. We know from scientists that the atom has nothing inside it. It is 99.99 percent empty. Thus, is science telling us what the Hindu Upanishads told us: all comes from Nothingness? There is a story in the Upanishad: the Rishi or guru asks his student to take a seed and cut it open. The student does so and says he took the seed of a great banyan tree. He cut it open, there was nothing inside it. He said to the guru the seed has Nothing in it. There you see now, in those deliberations of our ancient thinkers the idea of things — the universe, being self-existent, self-created — existed.

Now let us see what Stephen Hawking said: 'No one created the universe. As long as there was gravity, the universe would create itself.' In a creation that is self-created by its own forces and energies working on each other, there are many things happening all at once. One reaction moves to another, one cause leads to an effect and another cause. These are not metaphysical truths but truths of the cosmos where matter was created from energy, from Nothing that was material.

So these are some thoughts that churn up the mind. They must bring us humility. Because the Truth we have been speaking of has created us and everything we are: body and mind. We are part of that Truth and that Nature that is our highest consciousness. We cannot get behind consciousness; we cannot stand aside and look at that of which we are a part of. We must seek to know and explore so that we understand ourselves and everything better.

Bill
What was before the Big Bang? Our perspective creates our reality. When we are in a room, our reality is limited to the space within the room and the articles in the room. Imagine ascending now — against gravity. What do we see? We see the floor of the room as never seen before. Then let us crash upwards into the ceiling of the room and

pass through it; our reality changes. And as we keep rising, we crash through the roof of the house; reality and our experience changes. As we keep rising like a balloon, our perspective changes and starts broadening. We first see our whole house from above, then other houses in the neighbourhood, then our suburb, then our city as never seen before. Nothing is new but we had never seen it before at one glance from above.

As we rise to the altitude where planes fly, we hardly see any houses or anything below. All things become too small and hazy to be seen with our naked eye. Instead, we see a new reality — a portion of the earth, horizon and deep blue sky; all those earlier realities fade into insignificance.

After a while, as we keep rising into the stratosphere and ionosphere and then space, the whole Earth looks like a ball. Our realities keep on changing as our perspective keeps changing,

Now close your eyes and imagine seeing the whole solar system, with different planets rotating around their axes and revolving around the sun, with their little moons orbiting around them. You can only wonder: how is this all so balanced and in a stable equilibrium? There must be one system that keeps it the way it is! But then it stops there, as there are numerous solar systems in the Milky Way.

I am not able to conceive much beyond our solar system. Anything is possible, anything for that matter. But it is still stable. It is still coherent. Is it all coexisting by chance — by random chance? If the Big Bang really happened, then everything must have been embedded in that *one single point*. If the Big Bang did not really happen, then many questions arise. The possibility of the Big Bang provides limited closure to the query. Even my imagination does not take me beyond our solar system. I don't know how and which laws work outside of it.

Truth, we shall always search for you. Perhaps there are many truths and not one Truth! Who knows?

Chapter 6 THE TRUTH AND NOTHING BUT THE TRUTH

Vijay

We have talked about possibilities. The basic point being no one knows the Truth. So we must be humble and keep our minds open.

Bill

I feel sad and extremely small that my world becomes limited to my solar system. My imagination and mind are limited to within its boundaries although I have heard astronomers have found many planets beyond our system. And I have seen the Milky Way at Tekapo, New Zealand. I just marvelled when I saw it there. It is a long dust trail of stars.

Vijay

One Truth or many truths, we must live in awe of all this around us. As you so enthusiastically said, 'Truth, we shall always search for you', we, who are here, and those who come after us.

Bill

I recall how humbled and mesmerised I felt when I looked up, in disbelief, and kept watching the Milky Way on that midnight of July 2019 at Tekapo. If our Earth is such a small dot in the cosmos, what are we?

Vijay

That is what Carl Sagan said: 'We are a small pale blue dot in the huge canvas of the cosmos.'

Bill

I would like to conclude this chapter with a warning to humankind: When we get tunnel-visioned or blinded by 'our' Truth, all 'other' truths that we disregard — deliberately or inadvertently — sooner or later combine and devour us. Our paranoia and obsession with our

Truth lead to our ultimate downfall. No one's Truth is greatest; Truth is not big or small. Everyone's individual Truth is real and valid in equal measure.

Chapter 7

THE GOD IDEA

How we make our gods in our own image

We have had gods and goddesses as far back as there is a history of humankind. Not much is known of humans or their gods before 5,000 years ago. It seems certain, however, that humans have always looked to the skies and looked for a God or for a number of gods to save themselves from things that they could not understand or felt threatened by. The gods are all made in humankind's image. Berkley said if horses had a God it would be a divine horse.

We are continually learning more about ancient human life. It seems certain, however, that humans have always looked to the skies. For example, Australian Indigenous groups believe in the 'Dreamtime' or 'Dreaming' for at least 60,000 years. They believe, during *Dreamtime*, the ancestral spirits emerged from the earth and descended from the sky and walk on the land that they created. They created the landforms (rivers, mountains, forests and deserts) and all the people, animals and vegetation. After completing their work on the earth, the spirits returned to the earth and the sky and merged with animals and rivers and land formations. Australian Aboriginal people believe the spirits are 'alive' in them.

Vijay

I think the God Concept or the Making of the Gods gives us a chance to look at the God idea in various cultures, including our own. I think the earliest God ideas were that of the fertility or mother goddess. How indeed did humans make up their gods? It is quite interesting; they looked to the source of life. The Maya worshipped blood, they pulled out the still beating heart of sacrificial humans and offered it in the altar that was smeared with fresh blood. With the Hindus, it was the phallus. Gods fall in and out of popularity. Jai Santosh Maa was an unknown deity till a few decades ago. A film made her into a popular goddess. So it is interesting. God did not make humans in His image but humans made God in their image. So this can be good.

Bill

It will be an interesting topic. I think the first six chapters have laid a good groundwork in the lead-up to this core topic. The chapters following it should discuss the effects and fallout of the Making of the Gods. This topic, therefore, sits at the peak of an inverted V-curve. God is central to most, if not all, religions. Buddhism does not recognise God, which is unlike most other religions.

Vijay

Before I go into this discussion, I would like to share a thought from the French writer Voltaire (François-Marie Arouet, 1694–1778): 'It is impossible to believe in God. And it is absurd not to.' The ambiguity is quite devastating.

But I think it says so much about the strange certainty we have about the existence of *someone* who has never been seen through all the centuries, through the rise and fall of civilisations, but who has been worshipped and fought for and killed for relentlessly.

And it becomes even more amazing when one considers that the gods of humans have kept changing with the passing of ages. Our ancestors and their ancestors worshipped other gods with other names. They were worshipped in different ways but what has remained constant is the idea that God is supreme and all powerful and benign. Also, there have been, and still are, thousands of gods, but they all have the same attribute of divine power and supremacy. It is a strange trick of belief that we believe the impossible because we want to believe; we want the impossible for only that can set us free from our limitations.

As we go along here, it would be interesting to look at the gods we have had. At the same time we could mull over the thought that God is a primal need of humankind and, from age to age, has been perhaps our finest creation to symbolise the unknown, the infinite power, the beauty and the completeness that we seek.

Bill
I believe the history of mythological gods and god-agents goes back much before 5,000 years ago. For instance, as per the Christian belief — whose scientific veracity has been relentlessly pursued — Noah constructed an ark to save life and two of each of all species at the time of the great flood.

Hinduism — native to the Indian subcontinent — is believed to be the oldest religion in the world. Known also as the *Sanatana Dharma* (the eternal law), it comprises four major traditions: Vaishnavism, Brahmanism, Shaktism and Saivism. Their followers consider Vishnu, Brahma, Shakti (Goddess) and Shiva respectively as the Supreme deity. Most other Hindu deities are either related to them or considered as their incarnations (avatars).

As per Hindu mythology, Vishnu —the Preserver god of the entire cosmic universe — is believed to have many avatars — Matsya (the fish), Kurma (the tortoise), Varaha (the boar), Narasimha (the Half Man, Half Lion avatar), Vamana (the Dwarf), Parashurama (Rama with the axe), Rama (the king of Ayodhya and the hero of the epic Ramayana) and Krishna (the hero of the epic Mahabharata). Some people also believe Buddha (the founder of Buddhism) was the ninth avatar. It is also believed the next avatar will be Kalki, who is expected to appear at the end of the current age of *Kalyug*.

As a matter of interest, do the Vishnu avatars indicate the process of evolution? It is scientifically accepted that life on Earth started from the oceans.

Similarly, Brahma — thought to be the Creator god — is believed to have nine avatars: Valki, Kashyapa, Sukra, Kalidasa, Chandra, Samudra, Jamvanta, Agastya and Durvasa.

Shiva — believed to be the Destroyer god — is believed to have twenty-four avatars: Shankar, Veerabhadra, Bhairava, Khandoba, Nataraja, Ashwatthama, Ardhanarishvara, Muneeswarar, Muthappan, Pashupati, Gangeshwar, Rudra, Lingam, Dakshinamurthy, Ravananugraha, Vaidheeswara, Lingodbhava Somaskanda, Bhikshatana, Sri Manjunatha, Vaidhyanatha, Mahakaleshwara, Tryambak and Bholenath.

Tridevi — the Goddess of three worlds — is believed to have fifty avatars; Lakshmi has twenty-five avatars and Sarasvati four avatars.

So you see there have been so many avatars of gods and goddesses in Hindu mythology and there are possibly more yet to come, depending on what is still unknown or a mystery to us, and what is instilled in us. And all these avatars are believed to have arrived before modern history was recorded. You and I, and our parents and grandparents, and perhaps none of their ancestors have met them.

The question is: are these avatars real or imaginary? The answer may be: if you are a person of belief, they are as real as you are. So, there you go, whether fact or fiction depends on you and your belief. Fact or fiction is quite subjective. One person's fact can be another person's fiction, separated only by one's belief and others' resistance to believing. That is exactly how mythology differs from history.

What did Kashmir Governor Ali Mardan Khan see? Myth or real?

Chapter 7 THE GOD IDEA

Ali Mardan Khan (died April 1657), a Kurdish military leader and administrator, had served the kings of the Safavid dynasty that ruled Iran (1501–1736). In 1638 he surrendered Qandahar to the Mughals and took refuge in Delhi. The Mughal king, Shah Jahan, who is known to have built the Taj Mahal, honoured him at the Mughal court and appointed him as governor of Kashmir, Kabul and Punjab. Those days, Punjab stretched from Kabul to Delhi. In the capital city of Kashmir, there is a locality named after him, called Bagh-e-Ali Mardan Khan.[12]

Around Herath (Shivratri), Kashmir Pandits recite a popular poem on the Shiva in the Persian language, which is understood to have been composed and written by Ali Mardan Khan. Kashmir Pandits traditionally believe Ali Mardan Khan had a vision of the Shiva and Shakti while strolling in a Mughal garden, which had prompted him to write the poem.

The starting and ending verses of the poem are reproduced here from Vinayak Razdan's *Search Kashmir* blog:

Huma Aslay Maheshwar Bood
Shabshahay Ki Man Didam
Gazanfar Charam Dar Barbood
Shab Shahay

I saw him at night, I am sure it was Maheshwar
wearing a Lion skin on him, that night

Manam Mardaan Ali Khanam
Gulam Shah-e-Shaham
Ajab Israar may Beenam
Shab Shahay

---

12 R. Gandhi (2015) *Punjab: A History from Aurangzeb to Mountbatten*, Rupa Publications, New Delhi.

I, Ali Mardan Khan, server of King of Kings
I witnessed something very strange, that night[13]

This poem has survived and travelled down the generations of Kashmir Pandits since about 1650, perhaps initially by word of mouth — as per the traditions of the subcontinent — and later in a written form. It is up to you to believe it or not.

What is indeed interesting is that this legendary poem on Shiva is claimed to have been written by a Muslim governor of Kashmir of good standing, one who still carries a good name and respect among Kashmiri Pandits. There must be some credibility to the story. How could a non-Kashmiri Muslim governor have a vision, assuming he would have no prior belief or knowledge about the Shiva? Why would Kashmir Pandits invent a story and claim it was written by the noble Muslim governor and why not by one of their own in Kashmir? Why was it composed and written in the Persian language? These are some of the questions that we may not be able to answer at the moment.

As with many things of the past, the Truth remains elusive. It makes us struggle to discover it; it plays hide and seek.

The life extinction events of the past and present

Do you know the Earth has seen five major extinctions previously? The sixth extinction — called the Holocene or Anthropocene extinction — is believed to be already underway based on the extinction of many life species every day, although new species are also being discovered as we go.

Around 2.5 billion years ago, the Great Oxygenation extinction event was probably the first major extinction event. About 250 million

---

13 The blog post features eight verses that describe the Shiva. V. Razdan (2012) 'Ali Mardan Khan's Shiva Persian poem', *Search Kashmir*, 19 February 2012, https://www.searchkashmir.org/2012/02/ali-mardan-khans-shiva-persian-poem.html, retrieved on 11 January 2020.

years ago, some unknown catastrophic event happened abruptly — called the Permian-Triassic extinction or The Great Dying — that is believed to have erased most of life on Earth.[14] Subsequently, about 65 million years ago, the Cretaceous-Tertiary extinction or Cretaceous-Paleogene extinction event marked the end of the dinosaurs.

The Great Dying did not spare any life. Trees, plants, reptiles, proto-mammals, insects, fish, molluscs and microbes were nearly all wiped out. Life on the Earth had almost come to an end, with about 95 percent of marine life and about 70 percent of terrestrial life erased. The scientific reason is believed to be a catastrophic combination of severe volcanism, a nearby supernova, environmental changes brought about by the formation of a supercontinent and possibly the impact of a large asteroid. Palaeontologists are trying to find clues to the mystery of the Great Dying buried inside tiny capsules of cosmic gas within rocks that are believed to have survived from 250 million years ago.

It seems Nature has continually been creating and destroying life ever since life was created on the Earth about 3.5 billion years ago. Note that there is no evidence of life on the Earth in the first 800 million years of its formation 4.3 billion years ago. Is that the reason the ancient Hindus came up with the concept of the Holy Trinity to represent the three essential roles of Nature — Brahma (the Creator), Vishnu (the Preserver) and Shiva (the Destroyer), with Shakti (the Supreme Energy in female form) associated with each of the three forms? Once again, do the Vishnu avatars represent the process of evolution in line with Charles Darwin's theory? I'll leave these questions for you to contemplate on and answer if you choose to.

The creation of gods served many other purposes as time passed

God has always been a basic necessity for humans, in the distant

---

14 NASA Science (2002) 'The great dying', 28 January, https://science.nasa.gov/science-news/science-at-nasa/2002/28jan_extinction, retrieved 7 July 2020.

past and now. As the human mind has always been in search of answers — why, when, how, who, where, what — the only direction in which humans could look was upwards towards the sky, where the all-knowing God — the Omnipresent, Omniscient, Omnipotent — has been imagined to be sitting on a high chair, as we imagine a mighty king sits on a large throne. Since our evolution, we humans have intrinsically refused to accept defeat in cracking the 'mysteries of happenings' around us, despite realising our limitations. To reconcile with our limitations of the time, we cleverly created gods, with definite attributes and powers, for everything that affected our lives through time and about which we have had scant knowledge.

The creation of gods served many other purposes as time passed. There had to be One Mighty King, the greatest of all kings, who sat far above the Earth and was beyond our reach but could see everything that we did and at any time, and had all powers to defeat and destroy the mightiest of us and our mighty kings. This One Mighty King was necessary to make us feel humble and also make our earthly kings humble, as a check-and-balance system. We were afraid our earthly kings may possibly lose their heads in power and cause anarchy. God creation was thus necessary to empower ourselves and keep our kings in check.

Birth and death have always intrigued humans, even now. God had to be someone who controlled both, yet remained unseen. God had to be someone whom all humans had to report to and prostrate before. People were made to believe bad things would happen to them if they did not make God happy. So the necessity for the fear factor also contributed to the making of the God idea.

The portfolio of God must have logically expanded as humans started getting some answers and observing patterns in various natural phenomena. The more humans observed, explored and wondered — which must have happened in varying and different degrees at different times and different locations of the Earth — the bigger the God portfolio must have become.

Chapter 7 THE GOD IDEA

Have you ever wondered why we humans — from all religious faiths — intrinsically look up towards the sky when we look for God? The answer is we have nowhere else to look. We can't see with our eyes into the Earth. We can't accept the presence of God under the ground, below us. In relatively lateral directions, our capacity to see is limited by our vision and the presence of objects and obstacles both natural (trees, hills and mountains) and human-made. Intuitively, we try to look in a direction that is above us and seems to be clear, without obstacles.

We see the sun, the moon and those numerous stars, which are all up in the sky. We also see shooting stars moving across the sky. We have also found planets somewhere up there. We receive rain, snow, lightning, hail and sunshine from above. We naturally started believing the source of all these heavenly bodies and the elements of nature was somewhere up in the sky, or the ether, as described in the texts. That is why we intrinsically look upwards to the sky.

Due to changing paradigms, the God conception has also kept changing as per the demands of the time — to provide some explanation as to why many things happened. So I think God creations were a human necessity to provide some explanation of unknown phenomena.

Where humans could not think of a reason, a new god was created and named differently at different times and places. Even a local story was woven around that god, along with a local way of appeasing that god. For example, to explain earthquakes, it was said that the Earth rested on top of an animal (the World Turtle or Cosmic Turtle, or World Elephant or World Serpent) which caused the quake with its movement. For each of the elements and natural phenomena — rain, wind, fire, lightning and so on — a different god was created.

To conclude this part, humans must be credited with having an inquisitive mind to understand why things happened. Where no explanation was available, a god was created, one who knew how to and did cause things to happen.

Vijay

When I mull over what you are saying, Bill, I cannot help but recall Bertrand Russell's remark about religions that were created 'in the infancy of man's intelligence'. While I do not necessarily follow Russell in his strong atheism, I do think this remark of his has great meaning. The creation of the major world religions really did take place between 3,000 and 2,000 years ago. Humans knew far less, very much less than now. The sciences and all other disciplines of knowledge have grown tremendously. On that one basis alone, it seems obvious that the religious assumptions of an ancient age cannot be fully believed in today.

They made their gods according to their needs and imaginations at that time. That is precisely why the old gods go extinct. They do, as we have seen.

Let me bring you quickly to the later beliefs and religions. I point to a relatively modern faith like Sikhism that came into being about 500 years ago. In Sikhism, there is a Supreme formless God or Being and there are no mythologies, no descriptions or commandments. There are also no rituals except some that have been introduced for births and marriages, for example.

The Sikhs do have a holy book, the Guru Granth Sahib, which they venerate as a living guru because Guru Gobind Singh, the tenth guru, decided no human would heed the new faith. The holy book has neither theology nor didactic commands. It is a collection of songs and devotional verses created by the ten Sikh gurus and by nineteen other wandering minstrels of various faiths and of high and low castes — just songs. What I am pointing at is the idea of religion and its God has become simpler and more accessible as the centuries have passed. Much of the magic and mythology has disappeared. The God idea is very much there but it is a one-to-one experience for each individual human.

If you come to later religious and spiritual movements, you will see there is even more simplification of the God idea. There are no forms, no attributes to the gods of new faiths. There is only a concept of Supreme Intelligence and Energy. In fact, it is interesting that in traditions like Zen and other beliefs, of what is called New Spirituality, there is a divine essence, transcendence and a higher consciousness, which may be the presence of something godlike. But there is no God. This is perhaps a mark of the evolution of humankind's intelligence.

Bill
I concur. As knowledge unfolded — thanks to humankind's tireless endeavour to know —many aspects and expectations (gifts and punishments) and beliefs were gradually removed from the God portfolio. That must have been the reason why some gods had most or all their roles removed, as humans started learning about the cause and effect of those unknown happenings that intrigued them. The gods' roles became redundant, as humankind started knowing, leading to the gods' extinction. Knowledge led to the Truth.

You may draw a parallel between the scientific unknowns and the religious unknowns. Scientifically, we are still grappling with the concepts of origin and the creation of the universe — the Big Bang theory, black holes and so on. We are still struggling to know about the post-death journey and many other things. As long as these mysteries are not unravelled, religion and God will be followed.

As I mentioned in an earlier chapter, the scientific community knows very little about the human brain and how it really works. The research is happening and we are getting there, slowly but surely. The day we understand it fully, and why we die and if we can prevent death, the idea of God may become completely redundant, except we may still need God to save and defend us natural calamities.

Just reiterating, the idea is God will live on as long as we don't crack the unknowns — the mysteries — about the origin of the universe and about life and death, and find cures for all cancers, and a way to make humankind immortal.

The key to human immortality may change the whole paradigm.

What are humankind's greatest fears? Disease and death! The day we conquer them, the whole belief system will change. So the greatest question of all: can we ever conquer disease and death? So long as that does not happen, the God idea shall live on. And rightly so!

Nature and natural disasters will also keep reminding us about some unseen force that brings death and destruction on the Earth from time to time and against which we may be helpless forever.

Vijay
Yes, I think you make a good point. That if everything is known and if all the questions and the mysteries of life itself, and also the mystery of death and the afterlife, are somehow solved, then we shall not require our imaginings of God. But I do not think that is ever going to happen. Not because we will not try, or because it is impossible, but for the simple reason that it is our partial knowledge and intelligence that can never understand or know the supreme and the full intelligence of the Supreme Creative Principle.

That having been said, there is also the idea in my mind that our arrogance, our stubborn belief and efforts to tamper with natural laws and phenomena, such as genetic engineering, bring us into conflict with the forces of life and Nature itself. There is research being done to free us from all disease and from there to go on to achieve immortality. Billions of dollars are being spent and will be spent in the next decade to achieve these goals. They may or may not succeed. What I am trying to say here is that we may achieve any amount of technological and scientific progress but the basic human being — the body, the mind and the consciousness — has its source and nourishment from Nature alone.

The need for God and, as I have been saying, the need for new gods, will always remain. Consider for a moment that, with all the technological and scientific progress that we have had, humankind is still

Chapter 7 THE GOD IDEA

alone, helpless against human weaknesses and beset with even greater conflict and human injustice. That is the position today. And that is why we are still making new gods.

It will be the worst possible thing if one of the new gods that we make now will be the God of science. It will only aid our self-destruction.

The sublime and the ridiculous are both represented in the making of our gods

When we use the term 'God-making', it is no part of our intent to diminish the position of importance of the gods. Nor is it so when I ask where have the older gods gone.

We must understand that the need for a God figure and the age in which that God is created are both factors in the process. Every image and concept of a God is a metaphor from the myths and fantasies of a society in its own time. In the eras of great wars and strife, there were gods of war and power, gods that struck down enemies with thunderbolts, and gods that brought fair winds to armadas of attacking ships.

From those ages of wars and conquerors, we come to our own age where there are gods that specifically bless new Mercedes cars (for example, in Bengaluru, India), gods that seem to facilitate the birth of male children, and even gods and goddesses that look like movie stars.

The sublime and the ridiculous are both represented in the making of our gods. And this is not just with reference to polytheistic religions, like Hinduism. The major monotheistic religions, like Christianity and Islam, do not have specific gods for specific tasks. But they have specific patron saints and angels and even djinns to do the same sort of work, to fill the same sort of needs.

I think humans with a certain need or wish just create a helpful force for themselves. And it becomes a kind of reality that becomes bigger than them. I recall a guru or godman being asked if the Hindu deity Lord Shiva was real. I was there at this meeting of devotees and the guru. And I thought to myself that it was a tough question, very tough indeed for it asked if the God really existed.

The guru, as it turned out, was very smart indeed. His answer was: 'Shiva is more real than you or me. He exists not in flesh and bones that die out and are destroyed but in the spirit, in the essence of reality.' It was a good answer as it confused the devotees even more. Very often what we don't fully understand is also made sacred.

Bill

Here too, I concur. Recently, in Mauritius, where I was attending an international conference, we had a day out — organised by the hosts — to explore the host country. We were taken to a few Hindu temples, which contained two gigantic statues of Lord Shiva and Mother Durga as well as Ganesh and Kartik (Murugan).

All of a sudden, I found myself explaining to a number of delegates the metaphoric meaning of those symbols and attributes of the towering deities. The statues of the Shiva and Durga appeared to be nearly 100 feet high or more. I could not believe my ears what I was saying, based on what I have read and heard all my life. I could decipher so many of those symbols and attributes. The listeners got more and more intrigued and interested as I kept speaking. I said each deity represents an unbound ocean of knowledge, which is why Lord Shiva is known also as the Neelkanth and why he has a serpent around his neck, for example. Why does Durga have eight arms? Why does Ganesh look like that and why is a mouse considered to be his vehicle?

I was speaking extempore — spontaneously — as I'd never done before. I surprised myself. I did not see the revered deities as humans or images but as unbound books of messages, attributes, metaphors and knowledge.

For a moment, I loved my origins and how fortunate I was to have been born in a family where I got exposed to the deities and the concepts of their symbols and attributes. My life's learning has released me from a mental prison, transforming me from a mere surficial believer to a more humbled man of realisation.

I agree with you that those symbols, images and attributes of deities tell us so much about us, and what this universe and life are all about. It is simply brilliant. And, please note, there is no one rigid thought they reflect. One can draw one's own understanding of it all, while leaving one's mind open to all other alternative possibilities.

I do humbly concede that religion and the God idea are very beautiful concepts. To me, they have made me inclusive, perhaps because of my deeper, conceptual insight into the mythological stories and God attributes. The two great epics, the Ramayana and the Mahabharata, are simply brilliant and so relevant to humans and shall remain so forever, in all walks of the human existence: personal conduct, morality, ethics, the importance of education, social responsibility, the king's role and what not.

I love the messages from Ganesh and the Shiva, quite profound. But as I said before, one needs a deeper understanding of the concepts behind each deity. Once you get that — if fortunate or destined to do so — you become free. You come to the acceptance of all possibilities of the Truth and an infinite, unbound form of the Creator, as the Sikhs believe, the Nirakaar. One becomes liberated.

True liberation comes from knowing one is too finite and insignificant to even conceive the notion of the Infinite, the Indeterminate, the All Inclusive, the Within and the Without.

Vijay

That was wonderful to hear — your experience in Mauritius. I suppose your entire cultural background of family beliefs and your own understanding of Hindu traditions came into play. It made me smile when you said that your own knowledge of the mythologies surprised you. And you were so right. An Indian and a Hindu myself, I have access to all the modern and international ideas, but somewhere in the background, the old culture and the mythologies are always there.

I do empathise with the feeling that the mythology fills huge gaps of doubt and emptiness in us. This is not only in the case of the Hindu but I think it works everywhere, even though it is subconscious in most modern people, in even the most westernised cultures. There are stories and mythology everywhere. It was the way humans everywhere had to wish, to create a new and comfortable reality and to imagine a better world for themselves.

However, quite characteristically I suppose, I still would bring a word of caution here. We must understand and accept, at least today with all the information and the internationalism that one is supposed to possess, that the old cultures and mythology is beautiful and comforting, but they are mythology. They are stories made up by humans to be told in families and groups and around fireplaces in the old times. Like many things that we believe in and which are part of our lives, they are imaginings, tales of heroism and miracles. They are not facts.

We have all the great and powerful gods but it had happened and probably still does that, in times of danger or adversity, people go to these powerful gods for relief and succour when, in fact, they should be taking steps to face and overcome the adversity.

You see, Bill, we must understand the kind of wonder and appreciation a person like you, educated, modern and with an international worldview, has for mythology. At some point, you also know that these are beautiful stories. This is very different from a kind of complete and blind belief in the stories and mythology, where we see someone in India like a popular member of the legislature, an MP, saying that a great *yagna* or ritual prayer should be held to appease the mythological Indian god of rain, Indra, to ask him to bring the monsoon to a parched land.

Stay with me a bit longer as this is priceless. Sure enough the huge and very expensive *yagna* was held in that state where the rains had fielded that year. It was also part of a mythological story that if the marriage of a male and female frog were to be performed during the puja, it would please Indra. So this was done.

As it happened, we had a good monsoon last year, which is when the story took place. There was too much rain, causing floods in the state. So it was a reverse problem. Some more very knowledgeable and wise people then came up with the idea, again picked up from mythology, that since Indra had become too happy and had overdone it, what should be done now was to perform a ritual divorce of the frogs.

If you are laughing already, stay a moment more. So a puja was held again, and mind you, this was done in a modern state in 2018. With great pomp and participation from the elders and most eminent citizens of the city, the two hapless frogs were officially *divorced*. The rain and floods, of course, took their own course and, after the monsoon was spent, the entire crisis ended.

I have related this story, which was reported in all media, to show that mythology must be taken with love and appreciation for culture but the moment it is taken to be factual then that is a very big problem. The gods of mythology are important to us as part of our cultural consciousness. But they belong to a different realm now.

Before I conclude, I must also say this. We should understand the importance of mythology and of the gods. There must be belief, but there must also be discrimination and wisdom. Modern humans have another problem today. There are no mythologies. We do not have the stories that would give us a divine beauty and a transcendental meaning. This is something to think about.

Bill
Very impressive! Beautifully thought and explained, Vijay. You were very right; I could not stop laughing for a long time. In fact, my dad heard me reading it aloud and laughing. So I had to repeat the whole thing to him, while still laughing.

On a more serious note, however, imagine the world without these deities and the colourful mythological stories woven around them in the texts, and those beautiful mythological stories transmitted verbally in our homes of the past, perhaps some even now, which we would, as children, hear from our grandmothers with our imaginative little eyes closed during those long power outages in winter months, and even with our open daydreaming eyes fixated on the face of the storyteller. It would have been a very dull and boring childhood, simply bland. Culture has a special niche for mythology if it is vibrant, lively and educative, morally and ethically.

I do agree that a problem can arise when we can't see any difference between the reality and the myth because, in such a case, our thoughts potentially become rigid. Our beliefs clash with those who challenge them. Invariably, we feel offended and frustrated when we fail to provide any logical explanation or evidence to support what we say when we are challenged. In most cases, we get labelled as superstitious, delirious and backwards. And we react more. Many consciously adopt a rigid stance in defence of their beliefs to the extent they become aggressive. And what does it do? It polarises the community, as us and them.

Vijay
I think the story of the marriage of frogs to get rain is really symbolic of what is happening today in India: the rise of crass ignorance, a kind of willing suspension of intelligence, and *vivek* (discrimination) by people who are educated and otherwise quite modern. Why, you might ask? Because they are now aggressive about what they think is their cultural wisdom. It is not theirs, of course. The wisdom of the Hindus is in texts that these people will never read. So they push an ersatz culture, which might have belonged to folk traditions. It is dishonest and naive.

I do go along with you on the great value of our gods and mythologies. We agree that there must be balance and awareness. I mean, it is like Santa Claus. It is taken very seriously as a commercial and cultural myth. Its followers know, all of them, that it is a lovely tradition and a story. Now even the older kids know. But they enjoy it. It is like novels and films we enjoy. We know they are fiction.

Our gods are real only in our minds and in the way we give them our devotion to lose ourselves — to lose our ego and 'I-ness'. They keep changing and we make new gods but the One Supreme Intelligence of Nature and the cosmos remains as it is. I don't really think that we will have any more of those colourful, fantastic, magical mythologies in our modern world. Science and the knowledge explosion have made us cynical and very practical.

The same goes for the gods that our new belief systems will have, if indeed they do. Science has opened up our eyes to laws and truths but closed our windows to imagination and myth.

I think what we are seeing is that spirituality and science are pushing the world from the one side and a growing aggression of religious belief is pushing back from the other side. I think the two streams will always be there.

God is a serious matter in all religions. He is an angry God, a God who judges, and a vengeful God, also a benign God in adversity, a God to love. I think only in India we have, as the beatnik poet Allen Ginsberg once said on a visit to India, 'such easy, playful gods'. The Hindu gods and their stories are like those of our friends, magical friends. Be it the formless, monotheistic Supreme Intelligence or the gods of our mythologies, we should celebrate our gods and experience the joy of being close to the Infinite in our lives.

Bill
Yes, exactly, we are witnessing the survival phase of religion in the face of scientific thought. As science demystifies many theories and deconstructs many fears, many benefactors from religion feel threatened. Can we say science is threatening religion? Yes and no, both.

A religious belief may melt away just as a slab of ice melts when the knowledge of science, like the sun, emerges from behind the clouds of ignorance. In such cases, religion is threatened by science. But where a religious thought is a commonsense, ethical or moral message, a beautiful story — without any promise of heaven or fear of hell — it has no reason to be threatened by science.

One of the reasons why religion is seen to become rigid, as time passes, is its commercial aspect. Religion has become a big business for many stakeholders. Just like any other business, its proponents will do everything to maintain its unique identity — corporate, retail, wholesale, educational — when facing competition from peers.

Coming back to God as a Supreme Being, I have always maintained Its omnipresence — within and without— in our minds, as that is the only medium wherein we can silently pray and connect. For me, it is inconceivable that God could be anything different from us or away from us, sitting far above us. Scientifically, the 'above us' would mean an infinite number of directions because our Earth is more or less round, almost a sphere.

Yes, the Supreme Being must exist in its own Creation, including within us humans — its self-acclaimed (but not necessarily true) most intelligent creation — and act with all its attributes through us humans as well as through all its other life forms. This possibility provides the basis of the only plausible theory about the existence of God, one that can meet all three vertices of the charmed triangle that we have been talking about — science, religion and spirituality.

God must be omnipresent and formless (*Nirakaar*), self-correcting, all-encompassing and all pervading — within and without all Its Creation — following Its own natural laws. It is indeed through the discovery of Its laws, via philosophical and scientific means, that we should be able to realise God. Therefore, the more we discover through science or through deep contemplation and a deeper study of Nature, the more we should be able to discover God. In that respect, thus, we may call scientists God's own children, much more than those religious gurus and priests. That is what Swami Vivekananda said in the Vedanta.

Note that I have used the term 'It' as a pronoun for God and not 'He' or 'She'. In Its formless, infinite, all-pervading existence, it does not seem right to bring It to our finite level and give It a gender. Having said that, if one wishes to conceive It in any finite shape or form — any gender — that is equally acceptable. Everything is possible.

It looks rather intriguing to me how this book has just created itself — bizarre! The Central Station controls and regulates. Windows, doors and valves of the mind open due to some remote control.

Vijay

You are so right. It just wrote itself. We are humans with human minds and search for reasons and causes and DNA. But what really is to be comes out of nothing by itself.

You see we say a boy has this DNA and this genetic background and so he has this mind and this talent. We can fit the questions into our answers. But that talent, say, of being a poet or painter, that talent of thought and consciousness and emotional intelligence, it is not written in DNA. It is the Divine Intelligence … Oh God, there I go again.

Chapter 8

WHEN OPTIMISM FAILS

Does God really do everything for the best?

It is a fairly universal saying that God does everything for the best. It is a very comforting thought, a pious cliché. But does it really work that way? There is so much that happens that is terrible and cruel.

Bill

In late December 2019, a young voluntary fighter in New South Wales (Australia) tragically lost his life while fighting bushfires. He is survived by his young, pregnant wife. They had dreams. As a voluntary firefighter, he was doing good Karma. Did he deserve to die while trying to help others? Did his wife and his unborn baby deserve to lose him?

As of 12 January 2020, twenty-eight people were reported to have lost their lives in Australian bushfires since the fires started in September 2019. In addition, ecologists from the University of Sydney believe the Australian bushfires of 2019–20 have claimed the lives of 480 million mammals, birds and reptiles, including 8000 koalas, which is one-third of the entire koala population in New South Wales.[15]

In January 2020, 176 people died in a Ukrainian plane crash when it was accidentally (unintentionally) shot down by an Iranian missile.

---

15 R. Sadler (2010) 'Australia bushfires: 480 million animals, 8000 koalas killed by fires – experts', *Newshub*, 12 January, retrieved 13 July 2020, https://www.newshub.co.nz/home/world/2020/01/australia-bushfires-480-million-animals-8000-koalas-killed-by-fires-experts.html

Chapter 8 WHEN OPTIMISM FAILS

Iran admitted the human error and apologised but does that bring back those lost lives?

Where is justice? Is God behind all this? Is God kind? Is God always kind? We leave the readers to think and answer these questions.

Does the balm of belief fail?

Vijay

It is wonderful to believe in that universal saying, *God does everything for the best*, and to apply it as a balm to the heart and the body but it is also necessary to face reality. For whose 'best' do the terrible things happen? These are some thoughts that call into question the benign attributes of our gods.

Can we look all around us at what happens to people — the accidents, the disease, the tragedies of life, for example, all that you have mentioned above. Is it all really for the best? Cataclysms of nature that cause hundreds, even thousands, of casualties; the horrors of war, and riots and terrorist actions, so many things that hurt us, destroy those we love and destroy us. Who can really believe that all that is for the best? It is wrong to say a benign God creates these horrors of war, terrorism and human cruelty. Humankind is responsible. Let us not bring God into it.

Bill

Do we have any other option than to be optimists? Do we lose anything by being an optimist? A pessimist suffers the whole time but an optimist suffers only when things turn pear-shaped and tragic events unfold. And that optimism is usually bedded in our faith in something higher than us — such as God — who we believe watches us, guides us and protects us but only if that Higher Being is our guardian angel and, more importantly, happy with us. Where things do not turn out as per expectations, we blame ourselves but not our guardian angel. We place all fault on us — on Karma, on Destiny.

It is logical to expect that a stable state of equilibrium must follow instability. So if stability is a logical result of an unstable condition, it won't be unreasonable to declare God does everything for the best. If not, blame your Karma or Destiny, but not God. Once again here, the God idea comes into the picture.

And I believe that intense and single-minded focus on God, as some source of Infinite Energy, does help us to face our challenges. There may not be much provable rationale to this. There isn't. It is just a part of the mystery from which we can, and do, draw strength when we look up — from a murky darkness of our despair — deep into the infinite sky above us. The state of our mind deciphers the look of the sky — blue, grey or dark, star-studded — in different ways at different times. Looking up towards the sky seems to be a part of our intrinsic nature, involuntary at most times, with usually a look of wonder and hope on our faces.

Vijay
Optimism is necessary, of course, and the only way to live. So is the comfort of having a guardian angel. I am not so sure though that everyone believes the guardian angel pulls you out of hard reality every time. I think optimism fails us in real life many a time, especially if you are overconfident about the guardian angel. We have to learn to be alone, on our own. That is the hard stuff of life. And, more importantly, to take responsibility and do what is necessary to come out of the mire. *Whatever God does is for the best* is a kind of universal folksy wisdom that can be very comforting. These placebos of belief do help when you are clutching at straws in pain and depression.

We must never forget the thorns around a divinely blossoming rose

As Zadie Smith has said, 'If you wish to blossom like a rose in the garden, you have to learn to adjust to living with the thorns.' Things

Chapter 8 WHEN OPTIMISM FAILS

that cause pain and tragedy happen all the time. I am one of those who think God has very little to do with it. It is impossible to believe that everything that happens to trillions of beings on Earth is the handiwork of God.

We have certain laws of phenomena and in Nature, and those laws cause creation and destruction in their own course. There is something else to this. It is a human belief that we live in a benign and divine world. Bad things just happen. As I said, it is a presumption that everything from God must be good. We fail to realise that life and death, the good and the evil, is part of the same creation, by the same Creative Principle.

Humankind has always lived with adversity. It was worse in earlier times when certain technologies, like medical sciences, were non-existent. And we created our beliefs to cope with them. So many terrible things happen in the world that it seems just crazy to say they happen for the best. But I suppose when the chips are really down, that is when we look up to a God somewhere.

Bill

We humans generally create and try to live within the safety of our own imaginary, benign, make-believe world, ruled by the benign laws of a benign God. We like to see only the good part of Nature and, as ostriches, turn a blind eye to the destructive side of Nature.

The root cause of our skewed mind is our individual concept of God — as constructed by our elders, teachers and texts. We are made to imagine God sitting on a high chair, far above us — somewhere up there in the sky, invisible — but still be able to keep His eyes on us and listen to us. Not many are introduced to God through God's Creation and Nature. When the elements turn horrid and tortuous, such as cyclones, storms, earthquakes, avalanches, floods, landslides and forest fires, and people die as a consequence, we say it is God's wrath on humans and we are being punished for our bad activities, bad

Karma. We seldom accept the destructive side of Nature as it is, with all its unpredictability. It seems we don't truly understand the Shiva concept.

Nature levels everything. Nature does not tolerate activities that go against its laws and equilibrium. It becomes ruthless, blind and destroys. Nature is blindfolded; it is benevolent and nurtures equally, without discrimination. But it also does not show mercy or discrimination when it strikes.

I do agree there is some wisdom — an element of acceptance and humility, an element of hope, intertwined with optimism — in our self-hypnosis that God does everything for the best. We accept things as divine justice. Why? Because there is no other practical option! We move on; it is all about survival, we cling to hope. See how clearly we have constructed a reconciliatory support structure around us? We have created beliefs and theories of Karma, Destiny and a benevolent God. Just so as not to annoy God, and for insurance, we accept things and blame ourselves for all bad things that happen to us.

Vijay
You have said something of great importance in that Nature is blindfolded and does both what is benign for us as well as what is destructive. Nature does not care either way, as it runs by its own laws. Having said that, do we not have to also accept that Nature too is God's design and creation? So there again, we come face to face with the idea, unsavoury though it be, that when the cyclones and tsunamis and raging forest fires destroy life heartlessly, terribly, it too is the work of God or whatever is the Creative Supreme Power.

Those cataclysms of Nature are not for anybody's best. In the Hindu tradition of Vedanta, Nature is called *Prakriti* and we read in the Bhagwat Gita of a philosophical dualism: Nature is said to be the 'lower power' attribute of God. The higher attribute is the Supreme Self. So the physical material reality is a lower manifestation. The Supreme Self, the subtle Intelligence Consciousness, is the truth of the Pure Being.

This leads us to living in the physical world of Nature and its phenomena. Humans must experience both the goodness and the furies of Nature that exist by the laws given to it. There is no other way.

You also brought up a challenging point about our presuming there is a benign God. Bill, the truth is that, almost by definition, we think of God as good and benign. We do see there is a side to God of anger, of vengefulness for our bad actions and of punishing humans. These are the assumptions.

The storm, with raging winds and lightning and thunder, thus becomes an allegory of the wrath of God, also a display and proof of His mighty power. That is how we think. We cannot certainly have an evil God. So we have to justify destruction and suffering thrown upon man as God's punishment, His chastisement. You also mention that, in the Hindu tradition, the bad comes from our past Karma. I think these are just our human ways to explain away the tragedies that befall us and to still keep inviolate the benign majesty of God. They are assumptions and we just have gotten used to balancing out contradictions with such assumptions. The plain truth is that we are hurt and tormented and must accept that reality.

Bill

Vijay, unintentionally, we have created some contradictions. The Sanskrit word *Prakriti* is such a beautiful word and most apt in the present context. We all act as per our own *Prakriti* — our nature. For example, it is in a lion's *Prakriti* to hunt and kill other animals, but only to survive and procreate. Similarly, a snake bites when it feels threatened. A scorpion stings when it feels threatened. A female scorpion devours her male partner soon after mating, as do some other species. A moth consumes itself in a flame. A human falls in love and gets consumed. All *Prakriti*.

As for a benign God, we have practically no other option, it will become virtually impossible to imagine and accept a cruel God. We will lose all hope for a better future, and hope sustains life.

Thus, to survive and march on — till we are no longer able to — hope plays a great part and most of it comes from a benign god. Most importantly, it is only positive psychology that keeps us up and going. Negative feelings consume our energy and poison our body organs. For developing and sustaining positive psychology, a benign God is a must.

Here we go once again. We create our God — a benign and just God. We also create our own guardian angel, as we believe it is all about us and us alone. Everything we believe, we base it on our own psychological, physical and material requirements. These requirements define 'good' and 'bad' both. Anything that goes in line with our gain is good.

A story: two friends gambled with playing cards. Both of them needed money to meet some sudden expenses at home and hoped to win from the gambling session. As per the law of probability, one of the two gamblers won. He thanked God. The other one lost everything he had, he became much needier and more miserable than before; his wife kicked him out of his home. He cursed God.

Another story — my personal story: on 23 December 1989, the day of my exile from Kashmir, I waited in a queue for nearly seven hours for the confirmation of my flight tickets at Srinagar airport — from about 8am to 3pm — with my two-year-old son in my lap. My wife stood by my side. I was desperate to leave the valley. My earlier confirmed flight two days ago had been cancelled due to heavy snowfall on that day. On this day, however, first priority was to be given to those passengers who had the confirmed tickets for this day. On the PA system, a flight from Delhi was announced to arrive by 3.30pm. It was coming via Chandigarh. The waitlisted passengers started getting confirmed tickets but when I was just one person away from the ticketing window, all seats were announced to have been booked. I looked hapless. I had been standing in the queue for those seemingly endless hours — hungry, tired, fearful

— hoping and praying. I became angry at God but somehow did not move away from the window, standing resolute, hoping.

After about ten minutes, they announced another plane was on its way from Bombay (now Mumbai) and possibly the remaining wait-listed passengers could be seated on that plane. We waited, holding our breath, praying. The ticketing window opened about fifteen minutes later and, thankfully, we received three confirmed tickets on this plane. While we waited in the boarding lounge, I heard some passengers from the earlier flight saying their incoming flight from Chandigarh had been cancelled because the pilot of that plane had refused to take off from the Chandigarh airport due to bad weather. So only those passengers who had onward connecting flights from Delhi were transferred to this other plane from Bombay. All other passengers booked on the earlier flight had to return home.

As luck would have it, the incoming flight from Bombay landed safely at Srinagar airport and we boarded it and reached Delhi. I thanked God. Suddenly, my God had become benevolent for me.

Had I been initially lucky (and ultimately unlucky) to get confirmed seats on the earlier flight (from Chandigarh), I would have had to return home because our final destination was Delhi and we did not have any connecting flights to catch from Delhi. That night I concluded, from my own myopic perspective, that *whatever God does is for our best*. Imagine how I would have cursed God had I been made to return home, frustrated!

Vijay
Bill, the word *Prakriti* has to be clarified. I have used it as the word for Nature in Sanskrit.

The nature of the lion or the nature of the lover or a *sanyasi* would perhaps come under the 'modes' of Nature — the *Tamas, Rajas, Sattva* — the natures of beings. I think I remember Lord Krishna says this *Prakriti* is my 'lower' nature.

Yes, I had read that airport story in your book. I think these coincidences happen. In gratefulness, we thank God and that is good. But there is a larger picture of the cruelty of life.

Bill
I think we may have to allow and deal with such differences in our individual perspectives and understanding — to respect the spontaneity of the conversation. Well, let us negotiate it, as we do always.

Vijay
Much of folk wisdom and also the utterances of astrologers and gurus, who insist that God does everything for the best, is meant to soothe and heal. It is also meant to buttress faith in the ultimate generosity of God. And people believe in it because they want to. Many a time what these tellers of the future say turns out to be true. It is a law of averages. If they tell ten people that things will turn out for the best, at least two or four of the ten will have some good fortune. No sweat if there are still six who lose. The four who are successful tell the whole world that it was correct, that God does everything for the best.

This law of averages or coincidences has a high value in the world of religious and faith-based followings. People begin to believe that 'God knows best' or 'does everything for the best' when they see a spectacular, near-miraculous turn of good fortune in one or two cases. The other 80 or 90 percent who lost out are forgotten.

People believe in it too because sometimes it does happen that an event we thought was against our wishes turns out after some time to be in our favour.

There are many such examples. Someone who failed a medical examination went on to become a great writer. An episode of insult and violence turned Mahatma Gandhi from a career lawyer into a world leader for freedom. A rejected jobless JK Rowling had hit rock bottom in defeat and depression when she began to write the Harry Potter books.

Chapter 8 WHEN OPTIMISM FAILS

Things go very wrong for many people and then time and the momentum of the future take them to great success — those who believe there is divine justice and a divine plan for their lives. I will, of course, feel that coincidence, as has been said, is God's way of remaining anonymous. It is a feel-good kind of thing. And there is a value in that. Very often it is neither prudent nor pleasant to face up to too much reality.

Bill
Just look at our hypocrisy and myopic mindset. Consider an accident — a plane crash or a bus rollover — in which our friend or a relative survives whereas scores of others perish. What do we say when we hear the news that our friend or family member has survived? 'Thank God' or 'God is great'. But when we ask what about those who perished, what do we generally say? We say: 'It is God's Will' or 'It is their collective Karma'.

In addition to the stories exemplified by you, we also have stories of President Dr Abdul Kalam, who could not enter the Indian airforce, or the legendary actor Amitabh Bachchan, who made it big despite his initial struggles in the film industry. There must be numerous stories of misses and near-misses by people who failed and crashed, of deserving, brilliant people who could have shined but did not for reasons beyond their control. For a lack of alternative options to cling to, we start looking for a silver lining around the clouds. But tell me, how many clouds have you really seen with a silver lining? Perhaps sometimes when the cloud is small in size and has the sun right behind it.

You are so very right about the law of averages. It defines the mindset. Once again, I wish to emphasise that stable equilibrium always follows instability; there is no other third option. For example, if a person who has fallen from the top of a tall tree is precariously clinging on to a branch of a tree, what do you expect to happen at some point in time? At some point, either the branch of the tree will snap or the person's grip on the branch will loosen and give out. In both cases, the person will crash land on the ground and achieve equilibrium, albeit bruised and possibly injured. If the person does not suffer any major injury, we say, 'Thank God'. However, in the case of a serious injury or fatality, we blame Karma. In the case of a serious injury, we plead with God for mercy.

It is in us humans that we see things hypocritically, rather selfishly. As long as we or our person has survived an accident, it is fine. As a token of thanks to God, we also organise thanksgiving rituals and celebrate our luck. How often do we think about those who perished or their loved ones, their friends and families?

As a recent example of our dark, negative side and of our sadistic nature, our selfish retribution, many Kashmiris in Delhi, the National Capital Region and elsewhere in the world celebrated the lockdown of Kashmir and the abrogation of Article 370 in August 2019, which contained India's promise to Kashmir, as enshrined in the Constitution of India, to uphold its semi-autonomous status.

Ask any reasonable person why and the typical answer is: 'Why did they throw us out thirty years ago? Why did they remain silent then and in all those past thirty years?'

It has always baffled me how some humans can rejoice in the suffering of other humans. Perhaps they have never accepted the omnipresence of God. Perhaps they have never understood the meaning of *Namaskar*. Perhaps they have never moved beyond themselves.

How can we claim God is only ours and not of our perceived enemies? Why do we always see ourselves as victims and worthy of God's grace and special attention? I think the problem lies with our understanding of the God concept. The previous chapter should be able to address these questions.

How often do we thank God for tsunamis or cyclones or earthquakes that kill hundreds or thousands? We don't. But we also don't blame God for destroying us or for our calamities. We accept them as our Karma. If this is the reality, why do we need God? If Karma and Destiny define our life and our safety, we don't practically need God.

Yes, if God appeared and intervened in a similar way to how those comic-book characters do — the Phantom, Superman, Batman or Spider-Man — then we would have reasons to thank It. The concept of the Holy Trinity in Hindu mythology — Brahma (the Generator), Vishnu (the Preserver) and Mahesh (the Destroyer) — portrays all aspects of God, as do many aspects of the Goddess, some benevolent and some angry destroyer (for example, Chandi or Durga). I don't think God really does everything for the good.

Vijay, you have spoken about astrological predictions and folklore to soothe us against the effects of the onslaught from Nature, from God. Both these are meant to act on a relatively much smaller level (on us as individuals) and a much smaller scale (limited to a few people).

When we say God 'does' or 'does not' do everything for our good, we see ourselves as alone, as individuals, on a limited scale, such as in a house, a village, a city or even a country. God's act and its effect must, however, be seen on a much bigger scale.

Let us consider the hierarchy in the animal kingdom. Imagine those buffaloes crossing the African savanna. Have you ever felt sad for those animals, some of whom end up becoming food for the lions? But also haven't you felt sad for the lions when they age and can't hunt on their own due to their wounds and physical weakness? Those animals feed on one another. Otherwise they won't exist. On an individual level, God looks to be cruel, such as when a poor calf is caught and pounced upon by a great cat and made a meal of. Only when we see the bigger picture do our feelings change.

Consideration of scale is very important before commenting on the benevolence or cruelty of God. Are things to be commented on at a micro or macro level, or at an individual or cosmic level? Once again, the God concept comes into play. How large is the domain of God's activity?

Nature does nourish and nurture; Nature also destroys. Trees and grass are continually pruned and acted on so that they remain healthy. Similarly, natural calamities — acts of God — happen as per God's nature, on a cosmic level, and may be required for the overall good of the planet. Good and bad are relative and subject to the scale and level we look at.

Vijay
I think you have said it all in our attitudes and ideas of God's ways in relation to Nature. Things that happen are not always for the best of humankind. Nor are they for the best of other life forms.

I had the occasion a few months ago to see photographic coverage and video of the Amazon forest fires. I could see the animals in pain and torment and the throes of a death they could not escape. There were images of gorillas that especially jolted me. In abject fear and misery, the gorillas were seen staggering towards firefighters for help. They looked so much like humans.

In that moment, I saw a deep bond between the men and the scarred, desperate gorillas. They were in it together, two species of living beings tormented by the might of Nature. And then I did think that it was also true that both humans and gorillas are part of Nature. It meant Nature was destroying part of itself. I do not perhaps have enough religion and belief to assume or to reason that this too was some grand design of God and 'for the best'.

I do not think the destructions of Nature are always for the good. We can say that destruction is inevitable in Nature. But it is destruction nevertheless. It is painful, causes misery and burns up the very souls of living beings. It is cruel and unjust, at least from the human point of view. And that is the only point of view we do have.

Due to these cataclysms, there are millions of deaths starting from the smallest organisms upwards. Many species have gone extinct. Many communities of humankind, tribes and peoples have been wiped out.

Chapter 8 WHEN OPTIMISM FAILS

So then do the workings of Nature reveal the mind of God?

Does humankind, created of that same Supreme Mind, have to fight its way and fight Nature itself to survive and win through to life and happiness? It does seem so. I shall talk about this in a moment. There is another and even more important aspect to the torments of life and the world. This is the misery and ugliness we face, the pain of human cruelty and death in the unending conflicts and wars, the horrific tortures and inhuman barbarism of wars of religion where men kill for their gods. The world has been a terrible place too for the innocents who must suffer for no fault of their own.

Now there are two ways of looking at this. One is to blame it all again on God and the world God has created. All that misery then is the working of God. The other way is to blame ourselves; to my mind, that is the more honest and truthful way.

God does not cause wars. Humans cause them. It is humans who are cruel and barbaric. But then humankind too is a creation of the God power. So if we assume, as we do, that all is God's creation, then we must accept that the evil of humankind is also God's creation. And, indeed, what I said earlier is very true. More humans have been killed for God in religious wars than for anything else.

To blame God is a trap for those who are in the prison of belief and do not see reason. Our reverence and love for God must not flatten out rational thought. There was a Creation when humans and other beings were given life and a world to live in. Since then, they have acted by their propensities and according to how their minds work. We see them as parts of the Great Intelligence, as that is how we see the unexplainable and mysterious truth of life.

The primal spark of life and intelligence is what we may describe as the divine element in all beings. But in each individual that basic intelligence is being acted upon and modified and shaped by the senses, the thinking processes of a brain that is genetically formed like the rest of the physical body, and by the network of people around us. It was the existentialists who said that man was responsible. And, mind you, the earlier existentialist thinkers, like Heidegger, were believers in God. It was others who came later, like Sartre, who were atheists and said, 'man is condemned to be free'.

In my thinking, whether or not you believe in God, you still have to accept responsibility for what you do and what humans do. So it is not always a question as to whether God does everything for the best or not. Often the question also has to be whether humankind does everything for the best.

There we go again, Bill. You have been inspired too, I notice. Great.

Bill
Vijay, you have made me stand firmly — albeit uncomfortably, rather precariously — in front of the reality and I don't have much to say in defence of God, not that God needs me, a minuscule, for Its defence.

I may be able to raise some defence for God for unleashing natural disasters and calamities on us poor souls and get away with some curly explanation, but how do I explain all those human-made calamities — war and environmental disasters, such as the Bhopal gas tragedy (2–3 December 1984), bushfires, wilful negligence in design, construction and maintenance of modes of transportation (for example, the recent crashes of two Boeing 737 Max planes) or engineering infrastructure (for example, the Grenfell Tower fire in England, 14 June 2107), or the mass shootings every now and then, as in Norway on 22 July 2011 and the Christchurch massacre on 15 March 2019.

How can anyone say it was God's will that so many people — all innocent lives — became victims of wilful negligence or were the direct target of other humans, or does God do everything for the best?

I can't defend God in allowing these tragedies to happen and then watching silently. The only way I can absolve God of these crimes is to either (a) delink humankind from God — as we delink negligent employees from their bosses when things go wrong at a business, to save and indemnify the latter from accusations, or (b) consider humankind as part of Nature and one of the forms of God.

In the first case, God is made to look innocent whereas the human — Its most intelligent creation — is blamed for the deaths and suffering of other humans, and tried by law and punished as per law. God somehow gets away.

As per the second case, God can be blamed and accused, albeit blasphemously, for humankind's wrongdoings once we accept we are made in God's image and God acts through us. Can we accept this reality?

To me, the second case looks like a more plausible possibility than the first one. If no, then God has no role to play in human behaviour and actions. Thus, we are quite alone and independent in our thought and action, and, therefore, must be made accountable for whatever we do. In such a case, however, God acquires a much broader — cosmic — role only and has nothing to do with day to day actions on Earth. If so, we do not need God when we face calamities and suffer in the process. Humankind must act alone to help itself. If we are made in God's image, then God must accept the responsibility for everything that happens and equally share the blame for our wrongdoings. But, interestingly, on a practical level, while we may be punished under the law of the land, God will still get away because It can't be seen and arrested. In such a case, you may say God does not do everything for our best. Nevertheless, the faithful believers will never accept this scenario. Their explanation may generally be one or all of the following:

- There must be some higher purpose which only God knows;
- The poor victims had to face their Karma and Destiny;
- God tests us; or
- Who knows?

When we talk of babies and toddlers getting killed in war, or people getting killed in building fires or mass shootings, a weird thought flashes across my mind: that God is perhaps too busy watching a soccer match and can't be bothered.

Lastly, I agree with you about *Prakriti* being lower than the Supreme Self. God must be *Nirgun* and *Nirakar*, as the Sikhs believe.

In conclusion, humankind must be made accountable for its actions. I agree that the indestructible element of life in the human — the formless soul (the *Atma*) — may be a divine element that enters the body upon birth and returns to its origins, the Infinite Divinity (*Paramatma*), upon physical death.

In between, humankind acts alone, using mind and body, making choices and being free to discriminate between good and bad, and so on. Our *indestructible energy*, also referred to commonly as the 'spirit' or the soul' or the atma, is like a battery whereas the mind and body — software and hardware — are responsible for our actions. A battery can't be blamed for what kind of work a computer does, how destructive is its software.

I have surprised myself while penning down my response to your earlier thoughts.

Vijay
I am not at all surprised. For instance, just see how much both you and I have covered on these matters. I feel the mind and consciousness just open up at times. Yes, your response was well thought out and, what should I say, like a painter who suddenly knows what their painting should be. It is with me sometimes too, this oneness of thought and word. I think that is why we write.

Chapter 9

DIVINE VALIDATION – MAKING THINGS SACRED

Making things sacred is our way to believe

Everything that we must believe in is made sacred — customs, morals, behaviours, even thinking and even actions in the name of God. Humans tend to seek divine validation as a seal of approval and endorsement from the Higher Being, to support, justify and propagate their thoughts, beliefs, rituals, customs and actions.

Bill
Divine validation can be seen as something similar to the Agmark (in India) or ISO 9001 quality accreditation of products or professional services, as the case may be, to satisfy end-users that the product or services are of a certain standard. As per the laws of physics, water flows from one point to another due to either *gravity*, such as in open channels, streams and rivers, or due to *pressure*, such as in domestic water-supply pipes. Divine validation serves both as gravity and pressure in the justification and propagation of a thought or an action — a seal of approval. Alarmingly, sometimes a 'noble' end (subjective) is made to justify 'horrible and despicable' means.

Divine validation sells; it provides wheels and wings to our thoughts and actions. It also instils fear in us against repercussions in the form of punishment from an angry God if we oppose such thoughts or actions. Our resistance to any thought or action propagated with divine validation is seen as blasphemous and, therefore, considered a punishable act by the propagators and followers of an ideology or a socio-religious practice.

Divine validation flourishes and becomes effective only due to the ignorance — educational or otherwise — of the masses as well as their poor socio-economic standing, both of which are cunningly exploited by the propagators and perpetrators of a wrong ritual or a sinister ideology, using the mechanism of fear but all under a divine seal of approval.

Sometimes, when one's country is personified as a god or goddess, the term 'patriotism' too is misused, by some politicians, as divine validation to justify their actions against humanity. These politicians receive help from religious and spiritual leaders to seek divine validation. In doing so, they turn perceived and portrayed acts of blasphemy into treason, with dire consequences for defaulters, thus inducing fear.

Vijay
I am glad we are talking about this because most people in the world have always been convinced that God is endorsing every custom and culture and ethical system. It is fascinating sometimes to see and hear our priests and moralists tell you that 'this is what God wants'. How do they know is what beats me. And it is not just the priests, but also kings and rulers and commanders of armies have sent in thousands, I daresay millions, of men to battle to their deaths by telling them they must fight for their king and country and God. And sure enough, people believe it and are proud to die in the glory of war. In fact, there really is death and ugliness in war. God glory has been put in there because it was said God is with the brave.

I must share with you a small passage from that excellent book *Sapiens* by Yuval Noah Harari. Men go into battle, he says, on being

Chapter 9 DIVINE VALIDATION – MAKING THINGS SACRED

told that they will be blessed by God and go to heaven when they die for God and country. 'Even a monkey', says Harari, 'would not believe that.'

But humans have always done this and still do. We have terrorists called mujahedeen (or soldiers of God) who willingly, and with great religious fervour, blow up innocent people and also themselves. Because they are convinced, or have been convinced, and have worked themselves up to believe that *God wants that*.

It is not just the mujahedeen; warriors everywhere have been known to work themselves into a frenzy of barbarism for their gods, forgetting, of course, that hardly any God in any religion and scripture has advocated the maiming and killing of fellow human beings. But we and our ancestors seem to have willingly accepted this kind of divine validation of humankind's ugliest and most barbaric activity — war. In fact, it is amazing how many other patently unsavoury human activities are given divine blessings.

There have been criminal tribes in India which had their own specialised gods who, they believed, wished them to steal and despatch people to their maker by strangling them. These tribes of *Thuggee* (betrayal and theft) were declared criminals and hunted down by the colonial British. They still exist in parts of India. I located a group of these tribal *Thugee* in the badlands of the northern state of Uttar Pradesh during my days as a journalist. They were a living relic of the past in dress and customs. They were very proud of their criminal activities and said their goddess wanted them to steal and even kill as it pleased her.

The eunuchs, called hijras in India, also have their own goddess who blesses them. This goddess demands that when they die, their corpses be cremated in a standing posture. I mentioned these as some weird godly validation.

They exist in all old religions and societies. The most atrocious demands of humans are met and the guilt or moral factor removed by asserting that it is the will of some god or the other. And we do know that humans are quite adept at creating gods as and when they wish.

Bill
Vijay, you have perhaps raised one of the ugliest examples of divine validation — that is, in the name of their gods, humans have been committing the most heinous crimes against their fellow humans. Animals too are not spared and slaughtered as *kurban* (offering) to please gods. It baffles me how such people forget that their perceived opponents also follow the same maker or Higher Being, albeit with a different name. I believe divine validation is a necessity for getting a job done. It is commonly used for gaining wealth, power and exercising unquestionable control over other people.

Wars fought for religion or strategic interests — to defend or gain a territory, propagate a religion, subjugate people and exploit them financially and physically — need soldiers with strong convictions. Without divine validation, achieving such conviction is not possible. With such inspired soldiers, the chances of success increase phenomenally. This is the reason why countries have been portrayed as motherlands and fatherlands.

For instance, India is portrayed as *Bharat Mata* (Mother India), with the status of a goddess. When Indian soldiers fight, they believe they fight for *Bharat Mata* and their inspiration gives them significant courage and psychological strength. Even though they know, in the call of their duty, they will kill other humans in flesh and blood whom they don't even know or be killed by them in the battlefield, their conscience may remain relatively clean because they are made to believe they are fighting to defend their *Bharat Mata*, whom they imagine as their Mother Goddess. Their death is seen as their martyrdom and glorified. So are acts of 'bravery' wherein they may singlehandedly kill many enemy soldiers. This divine validation removes any sense of guilt that they may suffer from killing their opponents. Thus, such divine validation becomes necessary to fight war. It is for this reason that the

Chapter 9 DIVINE VALIDATION – MAKING THINGS SACRED

war cries of different army regiments have followed historical religious exhortations, despite the modernisation of warfare, for example *Jo boley so nihal, Satsriskal; Har har Mahadev; Jai Durge; Allah-u-Akbar*; and *Ya Ali*.

Humans still believe if they are fighting for God — albeit in their own imaginations — they are entitled to do anything, good or bad, to win the war and get away with their actions. Divine validation, real or imaginary, gives an unlimited licence to kill or inflict other violent harms, including the torture and rape. The end is made to justify the means, regardless of how criminal and inhuman those means are.

Anecdotally, in Kashmir, the religious mercenaries — *mujahedeen* from Afghanistan and other countries — would demand the local Kashmiris offer them their women — married and unmarried, young and old — for sexual gratification. The militants claimed to justify such an immoral demand because they fought jihad — a war to defend their religion. As such, in the name of their religion and God, they could ask for anything: food, shelter, money and women. And the local Kashmiris would find themselves in a precarious and helpless situation. They would not dare to refuse such horrible demands for fear of committing a perceived blasphemy (of not serving a jihadist) and getting killed in the process.

Imagine how Kashmiris must have suffered seeing their mothers, daughters, sisters and wives being used by those jihadists and in their own homes, in front of them and, of course, the suffering of the Kashmiri women themselves.

How can the world forget how the Taliban treated people, especially Afghan women, by degrading them to lower than animals? The same was done by ISIL/ISIS in Syria. Similarly, many Christian and Hindu priests and gurus are known to have committed sickening sexual crimes against men and women, boys and girls, while wielding the power conferred, implicitly or explicitly, on them by their religious organisations through divine validation.

Many rituals, religious and political, carry divine validation but mainly for the material benefit of the sick-minded and corrupt wolves in lambs' clothing who wield disproportionate power, influence and authority.

Vijay
Well, Bill, I do believe you have said it as it is from both perspectives. Some wars have to be fought to defend attacks and certainly soldiers are motivated by these beliefs. Wars are, of course, without exception, the forced tragedies of our lives as humans. History and our own current times tell us that humankind will always fight and will destroy life and Nature. The ideals of peace and harmony may never be achieved. It is not a nice thing to say but it appears humans are too stupid to prevent their own destruction and misery.

While you do point out that it is important to motivate soldiers to fight, whether for the right or the wrong, I would hasten to say that it is, in any event, just using the name of God to motivate people to kill and be cruel. Whatever the cause, people in their millions are given the amorphous promise of God's blessings and a place in one of the various heavens if they kill their fellow men.

And as you have so poignantly pointed out, in the case of Taliban fighters, in Kashmir, it does not stop at fighting and killing the perceived enemy. It goes on to rape and pillage and arson, it goes on to horrible cruelties upon women and children, and it goes on to the most inhuman oppression. It is all in the supposedly benign shade of divine validation.

We also know that wars are not just the fighting and killing of soldiers. In every civilisation – in different eras in different cultures and countries – there was terrible cruelty after a war was won or lost. After the war, and rape and plunder, men, women and children were taken into slavery. These slaves were human beings but were treated worse than humans treat animals and subjected to untold pain and misery. All of this was justified by scriptures of major religions like

Islam and Christianity. It cannot be explained with any rationality that God, any of the gods involved, would have wanted all this rape, pillage and plunder.

So you see, the scriptures and the belief systems have got it terribly wrong. Or, as I always emphasise, all scriptures were written to address the circumstances of the times in which their writers lived.

And I say without equivocation that, to use God and religion to justify, even to make blessed, these activities, is always wrong, maybe not from the religious or nationalistic point of view, but certainly from the point of view of humankind and humanistic values.

This is a simple truth. Whatever divinity we may believe in, the highest of creation, the ultimate mystery and miracle, is life — plant, animal and human life. Any belief that justifies the destruction of that divine presence of life is wrong.

Bill
Dear Vijay, I am in complete agreement with you. You have nailed it very well. If only we stupid humans could understand this thought, the world would be free from violence, pillage and the abuse of women and children. Nothing is more divine than life. Nothing can justify destruction of life, whether of humans, animals, flora or fauna.

So I believe and reiterate that 'God validation' is a simple trick that has worked historically and will continue to work until such time as we humans don't understand the reality of life and how some of us exploit most of us in the name of religion.

Have you noticed how religious leaders and directors of religious exploitation justify the results? They usually say: 'God tests us and our faith. God wants to see how much we love Him, what we can do to please Him and what we can sacrifice — ourselves or others — to make Him happy.' Such people see God as something similar to us — in form and mind, with our kind of ego and emotions — and one who enjoys testing and punishing us, as a sadistic being. And they are all wrong.

The most exploitation in the world happens in the name of God. Miseries are unleashed on others and justified in the name of God.

God validation requires mass support for achieving its effectiveness. Without mass support, it does not work. For example, God validation has gradually lost its ground in the Judaeo-Christian world, as science and proven knowledge have taken up an increasing space alongside the traditional belief system. With time, science has gained acceptance as the main source of knowledge, and religion relegated to a smaller role in a moral domain.

Some people justify the killing and eating of animals by equating them with vegetables and fruit. They argue if vegetables and fruit, which also carry life, can be consumed without any guilt or hesitation, why not animals? They claim animals have been created by God for human consumption. Some people also practise animal sacrifice, called *bali* or *kurban*, to please God. Animal sacrifice, even human sacrifice, has been practised by many sects of both Hindus and Muslims in exchange for saving the lives of one's dear ones, all under the seal of God validation.

Vijay

Let me put it this way, Bill. As you do say, this whole business of divine validation is a ploy and a manipulative stratagem devised by the *controllers*. 'Controllers' is my word for the few men, priests, rulers and commanders, who have called the shots on human history all through time. They are still doing it today, though there is much more individualism and dissent now.

Maybe that arrangement of leaders and followers is a work of Nature itself. It applies to all species, for good or for bad. There are always controllers. And these are the kings and present-day leaders of politics and religions who benefit materially from exploiting peoples' generally ignorance about the natural phenomena and environmental factors. These very few people dominate with their propensity to get power over all others.

Chapter 9 DIVINE VALIDATION – MAKING THINGS SACRED

It is a human trait of mind and body, nothing more. What I am getting at is there is nothing divine about this. But rulership has been made divine. The king is considered, or considers himself, next only to God. There, under the divine right of kings, a concept in the Christian nations but followed in essence everywhere in the world, a king was considered above all humans. And the priests and gatekeepers of religions endorsed this. The king had a divine right. So it was that all rulers, with the collaboration of religious leaders, could indulge every fancy or desire and commit any cruelty by their divine right.

Here I must mention the sexual proclivities of these bearers of divine right. Kings of all religions had hordes of mistresses and concubines even in societies where ordinary men lived happily with one wife. In medieval Europe and England, a strange divine right was devised for kings and rulers of principalities. This was called the *primae nochtis*. It meant that the ruler or ruling nobleman had the divine right to spend the first night of any woman's marriage with her, to the exclusion of her husband. The husband was supposed to consider this — another man sleeping with his newly wed wife —a blessing. I think it quite hilarious as a divine right, though I am sure it was a harsh reality for people then.

Weird and inhuman things were made sacred. In India, we know that the division of people into high and low castes and Untouchables, a horrible custom, was considered a sacred custom and divinely ordained. In Islam, there has been the custom, divinely sanctioned, of four wives and also something called contract marriages. A man could, by religious contract, marry a woman for a few days or even hours. There are other weird sacred stipulations. Some or most of them are not in any original scripture but have been added at will by clerics to the list of divine validation. Men just camouflaged their lust and greed with a false divinity.

Bill

Quite right, Vijay, I do agree. The classic case of *Triple Talaq* and *Halala* illustrate the dark side of men and how women have been exploited and abused in the name of God and religion.

Although the common explanation is that the practice has been devised to discourage *Talaq*, the ground reality is that the priests — mullahs — have exploited it to the hilt, for their own gratification. How? Only due to the power provided to them by their religion. [In the Islam, the word *Talaq* means 'divorce'. The word *Talaq* needs to be spoken thrice by husband to confirm his intention and set his decision in stone, which he can't revoke without letting the Sharia law take over his marriage. It gives him three chances to rethink his impulsive decision. Horribly, his wife has absolutely no say in his decision-making and the subsequent heartrending process that she has to follow and endure. Thereafter, if he regrets, he can't do much. The only way he can have her back as his wife is if she marries and sleeps with another man who must then divorce her so that she can returns to her former husband.]

The practice of religious leaders and kings, past and present, who have enjoyed status as a 'God deputy' to a lesser or greater extent is simply pathetic. But might is right and because God is considered to be the mightiest and greatest of all, humans have learnt to get the seal of approval from the masses by claiming they represent God and have His approval to do anything they wish to do.

Historically, kings in the Western world would be guided by the religious advisors — bishops — who carried the God seal of approval. The same was the case in India where a king, usually a *Kshatriya*, would be morally controlled and endorsed by a Brahmin advisor. In the Islamic world too, kings would be controlled and endorsed by imams.

Old gods are replaced by new gods as time goes on

Chapter 9 DIVINE VALIDATION – MAKING THINGS SACRED

History has witnessed the birth of the Anglican Church when the King of England, Henry VIII, refused to follow the Catholic Church and the Pope, and crowned himself as the head of a new church to snatch God validation from the Pope, which was necessary for him to divorce his first legally wedded wife and then remarry his new love, and continue lording over people.

Why does a common person prostrate before powerful people — politicians, leaders, gurus, the rich and famous, including celebrities — in the same way as they prostrate before deity? Power! People prostrate before power. And what is the best label of power? God!

Anecdotally, in India, there are temples of some famous film actors, such as Amitabh Bachchan, where their idols are worshipped daily. Such actors have acquired God status in the eyes of their followers. Why? Because these actors are rich and famous, and they act well on the screen in the virtual world, plain and simple!

In India, even Sachin Tendulkar is considered the God of cricket, a status which even the great Sir Don Bradman did not enjoy in his time. Now that Sachin has retired and the memory of people being short, Virat Kohli may soon be crowned as the next avatar or the God of cricket. The process, in people's minds, is similar to the birth of Vishnu avatars. Before Tendulkar, we had the great Sunil Gavaskar and Kapil Dev as gods of Indian cricket in their own time.

Indians love the creation of gods in everything they do and follow. So when Amitabh Bachchan or Sachin Tendulkar, and now Virat Kohli or Dhoni promote a certain commercial product on TV or on a billboard, the product receives God validation.

Vijay
Well, you have pointed to the consumerist way in which sports and film stars are used to brand and sell products at risk of being very facetious; I must say that the most successful branding of all time has been the God brand.

Countless millions down the centuries have 'bought' religious ideas on pure faith without having any way of knowing what is real and true. People need validation of some kind. That is the only conclusion one can come to. They do not believe themselves or what they think. That is where the controllers of opinion and thought come in. They guide the thoughts and beliefs of humankind.

I was going to talk to you about the most important of divine validations. It has to be the way in which men have made their religious texts infallible and sacred. Every religious text that is called a scripture is supposed to be a 'revealed' text or one inspired by God, revealed in one way or another from God himself directly to a prophet or a messiah who then delivered it to humankind. All this activity of scriptural texts seems to have begun the earliest in India with the creation of the Vedas about 4000 years ago. That is the earliest we know of our gods and scriptures. What existed in the religious or godly space before that is unknown.

The Vedas of ancient India were followed by the philosophical texts of the Upanishads, of which the earliest are known to have been created around 1200 BCE. They were texts first created in the oral tradition and later written on leaf and tree-bark materials. They are all understood to be revealed texts. Therefore, like all other revealed texts, such as the Koran, they are direct communications from God to human. The case of the Koran is one of the most infallible and rigid in revealed scriptures. Not a single word or accent or character of the words in the Koran can be changed. I know of a large printing house in Delhi which bagged a huge order of printing and producing a hundred thousand copies of the Koran. In spite of every care taken, one infinitesimal printer devil did manage to creep in; a hundred thousand copies were printed with one accent mark wrongly positioned. The entire order of a hundred thousand copies was rejected. All the copies were shipped back. The printing house did, of course, reprint a full form of eight pages, do another book-binding job and retrieve the situation.

Chapter 9 DIVINE VALIDATION – MAKING THINGS SACRED

But that is how sacred and unalterable the direct word of God is. It is interesting to consider, however, that God spoke in various languages native to the geographical area in which a scripture was written. They were taken down on bark or papyrus from oral traditions by humans. It is my belief they were highly inspired and wise people. And, indeed, that level of inspiration and creative intelligence may be well described as something divine or beyond ordinary intelligence.

The case of some of the Hindu holy books is also curious. Apart from the Vedas and earliest Upanishads, the most sacred book of the Hindus is the Bhagwad Gita. This is said to have been written by the Rishi (holy scholar and seeker) Ved Vyaasa around 500 BCE. The Gita is known to present the essence of the Vedas and Upanishad philosophy through a dialogue spoken by Lord Krishna. The dialogue was between Lord Krishna and the Pandava warrior Arjuna at the time of the Mahabharata war. Now here lies the problem. The Mahabharata war is roughly dated to 4000–3500 BCE. The Gita was written around 500 BCE, nearly 3000 years after that great war. Yet the creator of the Gita quotes every word as spoken by Lord Krishna. And every Hindu believes each word is indeed His word, the infallible and sacred word of God through his avatar or human incarnation, Lord Krishna.

The Gita is a profound book of philosophy. Its great importance, as one of the loftiest works of human wisdom, is universally acknowledged. But an additional sacredness and infallibility is sought to be given to it by asserting it is the direct word of God. It is not even necessary to give such validation to these profound works of wisdom. They stand by themselves as lofty works of human thought.

In fact, I agree entirely with the idea that they must also be read by people of other religions as literature and philosophy. They were truly the seed of evolving human thought that continues to evolve, seek and discover even today and will do so in the future.

Bill

You have raised some sensitive points about the possible time gap of nearly 3000–3500 years between the widely accepted Mahabharata period and the time when the Bhagwad Gita could have been written. The infallibility of the account given in the sacred text may indeed raise curiosity with a seeker but, on the other hand, a *believer* will not even bother to raise a brow. It is a similar case with the sacred texts of all other religions. Their infallibility renders them immortality. And that infallibility is founded on the unquestionable belief that they are divine and scared texts — beyond any question — and revealed to the man directly by the Divinity. The extent of infallibility is such that even this conversation between the two of us may be construed as blasphemous by some people.

On a relatively lower level, even the rituals undertaken at the time of birth, death and marriage in all religions carry divine validations. A common person is compelled to follow the traditional customs and carry out the rituals or otherwise face socio-religious backlash. In some communities, if the person challenges those rituals, the person may face social backlash and potentially end up becoming a social outcast. On the contrary, a socio-politically powerful or wealthier person may get away. People prostrate before power.

In my view, where masses are involved, you need raw material power in the form of wealth and/or political or religious influence to drive a certain action or a thought. Where that is missing, some form of divine validation will intervene and sort it out.

Divine validation sits unshakeably deep inside the human psyche. The indoctrination and grooming from early childhood is such that even most educated people don't dare to ask questions for fear of retribution. Fear provides wings to divine validation — fear of the unknown, fear of social backlash, fear of retribution and so on.

Chapter 9 DIVINE VALIDATION – MAKING THINGS SACRED

Vijay

Few things in human nature change, my friend, in spite of a vastly different and changed world today from what it was at the time of the birth of religions. That in itself, to my mind, demonstrates the stagnation of the religious belief. Religions are frozen in time. The fact that they don't change is their defining defeat in a modern world. We are now seeking more relevant validations for knowledge and ideas from science and logical thinking and, to some extent, from intuitive cum rationalised constructs of philosophy.

As for your earlier assertion that the beliefs of the masses of people will not change, I cannot but agree. Unfortunately, religion gives a bad choice: either you believe totally in it or you do not. As a result, we have been seeing a considerable rise in atheism or other systems of spirituality without God or religion. That is unfortunate because human intelligence works with both, reason on one hand and intuition and faith on the other. Having said that, all humans are not same and, to be spiritual, one may not need God at all. I also think the only real validation for modern humans now is to know that our thinking, reason and beliefs will help us live as more complete individuals and better human beings.

I think you did say at the start of this discussion, Bill, that divine validation also had a positive role in some cases. I would certainly go along with that phrase 'in some cases'.

We are critical of so many instances of divine validation in religions. That is necessary and good. Because, as I am never tired of saying, nothing is so sacred that it cannot be questioned. Questioning does not mean denial. It only means you are thinking it over and will accept or reject on merit.

Having said that, one has to say that the faith and self-confidence aroused by divine validation of some things is a strong motivator; it helps create a focus of will and determination. That is the positive role, in fact, of all prayer and worship: it brings an inner strength. It doesn't really matter if someone up there is heeding that prayer and will grant it. For that time of prayer, there is a self-projection into a larger reserve of energy and intelligence.

So then, the student before an exam who chants from the Gita, the Bible or the Koran, the person in distress or pain who hangs on to a holy amulet or prayer beads, and the person who faces impossible odds and obstacles with the name of their God on their lips, all are accessing that great cosmic reservoir of energy.

Of course, divine validation is a help in many cases. If it drives you to action, to near-impossible levels of struggle and to achieve goals that need to be achieved, a strong belief and its positive energy is a great force we can bring to ourselves. But in all cases, there must be awareness and understanding of what one is doing — of the human ethics. As you can see, I do not say religious ethics. If there is a divine validation in your religion for something that you think is wrong, then it must not be done.

Let me say, in conclusion, that the only real validation for modern men and women today is to know that our thinking, reason and positive beliefs will help us live as more complete individuals. And better human beings.

Bill
Thank you, Vijay, nicely summed up. The conclusion comes with very good practical, moral and ethical advice.

Chapter 10

INTUITION AND INNER KNOWING

Messages from the Infinity for us

This chapter discusses the mysterious human faculty of intuition — ideas, warnings, gut feelings, premonitions and intimations of what is yet to come to us. They seem to come by themselves and are invaluable sometimes as we take a step in the dark, into the territory of the unknown future. How does it happen? From where do they come? Who sends them? Do only some of us receive them or do they come to each one of us? This chapter explores these questions.

Vijay
We are interested in *inner knowing*, where we get out of the way of ourselves and become aware, opening our minds and consciousness to the messages of Nature, the vibrations of people and even places. It is a stage or a state of mind wherein we are in harmony with what is around us. The wisdom of knowing within one's being.

Bill
This topic — like Karma and Destiny — is one of the most abstract areas of discussion. How do people foretell, predict, foresee? What is the source of their information? Commonly, we call it a 'gut feeling',

borne out of 'premonition' or 'intuition'. What does 'gut' mean? My take on the word is that the 'gut' is a different organ to the 'head', which thinks and analyses, and to the 'heart', which feels, mostly in terms of love, affection and emotions.

Gut feeling could also be interpreted as catching 'vibes', as you have mentioned. That possibly happens if one is in physical proximity of a situation or a person of interest or a potential source of trouble. But how do we explain the uneasiness felt by a person sitting thousands of miles away about some person's health or safety? Are they dreams (or nightmares) seen by a receptor in advance of an event? How do we explain events foretold by soothsayers, spiritually high souls, seers and even common people? I can share several stories from my own experience as well as stories from others.

Anecdotally, my great-grandfather made a few prophecies. He was a moneylender and also a devotee of Goddess Kali. Among his prophecies were two about my grandfather and one about me.

It is said that on a cold wintry day, as snow was falling outside, he looked at the face of my grandfather intently for a while and made two prophecies. That time my grandfather was in his early thirties and a teacher at a high school at Anantnag, Kashmir, run privately by an Islamic organisation:

(1) *The world will turn upside down and you will be employed by government.* This happened unexpectedly when the school was suddenly taken over by the government of the day. Later, after completing a Bachelor's degree in education, my grandfather was appointed as the headmaster of the school where most staff were Muslims.

(2) *You will one day go to Ladakh and do good work there. Our ancestors lived and ruled there for generations.* This happened about two decades after the first prophecy when my grandfather was posted as headmaster of a government high school in Leh, Ladakh. During his two-year tenure, he won many awards, including one from Pt Nehru, the then prime minister of India, and one from Dr Karan Singh, *Sadr-I-Riyasat* (the then president of the state of Jammu and Kashmir).

(3) *Our seventh generation in Kashmir will significantly raise our family profile on a global level.* That seventh generation happens to be me, the only child of my parents.

Vijay
Well, what we are saying is that intuition or gut feeling is a faculty, a way of knowing, that we can't explain. Just one of the mysteries we live with. Psychologists say it is the subconscious and there are even quite a few bestsellers that claim they can teach you to use this faculty at will. I am sceptical though. Religious people say it is a spiritual thing, especially in India, but also everywhere else. Foretelling, answering questions about the future and so on are popular. However, once again, I am very sceptical. All this only panders to an almost natural yearning in all of us to know what will happen.

I do not think we can know. I am told stories of godmen and gurus who predict events and perform miracles. I have also met people who say a guru foretold an event or performed a miracle cancer cure and many things like that. I know they are earnest and honest, and I believe it is true; here I am less sceptical, though I still think it is not always true. I am less sceptical because some people have the wisdom and vision to read patterns of events and also to analyse the mental traits that affect an individual's future. As for curing cancers, I will come to that in a moment.

My considered understanding is that tremendous coincidences, even miraculous events, take place. But, and this is important, they happen by themselves in the course of Nature's ways. Most stories of miracles performed or jaw-dropping accuracy in foretelling are about events that happened in the natural order of phenomena, though they appear miraculous to us.

I go further with this line of thought. I do not believe that any human being can perform miracles or know the future at will. What I mean quite simply is that there are people who may have the gift and — in certain states of concentration, trance or prayer — be able to do or say supernatural things. But in most commercialised cases, I say it is a calculated con. One or two predictions out of a hundred are bound to come true in the natural course.

Those couple of predictions that come true make someone's reputation and the predictions in themselves also get a reputation. The other ninety-eight go wrong but are forgotten. But we are not so interested in astrology here, though you did mention soothsayers and foretellers. People do have strong intuitions sometimes, but I feel it is always a bit iffy to make very far-reaching decisions based on them. Of course, if you get an intuition and act on it and if you get a happy result, you are bound to believe in it totally.

If you think I am being unduly negative here, it is mainly because I have seen a great deal of suspension of disbelief in people blinded by faith. They just want to believe someone or they themselves are so desperate to know the future that they will believe anything told to them. Personally, I have known some very great spiritual masters, very few because such evolved people are very few anyway. And I also say such people exist all over the world, though not as gurus or spiritualists but perhaps very ordinary enlightened people.

I know of at least three such spiritual masters who were credited with having cured cancers and, if the stories are to be believed, they even brought some devotees who had died back to life. In all three cases, which included the great Ramana Maharishi and the Satya Sai Baba, the great spiritualists died of cancers. This is not just being negative or contrary, Bill. I just do not believe that anyone can have control over natural forces and phenomena. Prayer, positivity and strong good vibrations, as with autosuggestion, hopefulness and so on, can help with positive energy. But, in the final analysis, Nature will have its way.

As far as I go, intuition and inner knowing are deeply personal faculties. They are realised sometimes but they happen when they happen. They are tremendous faculties but I do not think they can be used at will. Of the two, I think what we are terming as 'inner knowing' is a more dependable, even a cultivatable, gift. It means, in my mind, a kind of deep wisdom that is the fruit of a lifetime of thought, meditation and being alone with yourself.

Bill
Quite interesting! I share your thoughts and theories surrounding (a) the law of probability, (b) inner knowing, (c) the human inability to override Nature and natural phenomena, and (d) the business of con artists.

You mentioned Satya Sai Baba. I know about a person who was virtually motionless and was carried from Kashmir to Baba's ashram on a stretcher, who returned to Kashmir in a wheelchair, talking. This person, a third-year engineering student, contracted meningitis and suddenly collapsed while watching TV. His relatives somehow managed to get a quick appointment with the Baba and the rest is history. Despite suffering from a serious physical setback and loss of time, he went on to complete his undergraduate studies and then postgraduate studies, purely with his own sheer determination to survive, stand and move ahead. Later, he took up a lecturer's post in the university for a while and finally moved on to take up a prestigious strategic job, while using crutches to walk.

In a contrasting case, this person's young uncle, a doctor, unexpectedly drowned in a swimming pool, but was resuscitated and kept on life support for about three weeks. Frantic efforts were made during those three weeks to get an appointment with the Baba, without any success. And he passed on. These cases illustrate one's ability to override Nature. In hindsight, it seems the first person was destined to live on and perhaps Baba knew that. Accordingly, Baba would have agreed to see him. Unfortunately, the second person seemed to have reached the natural end of his life. Perhaps Baba knew it was futile to do anything.

Vijay

These are very interesting anecdotes indeed. And I believe this kind of intuitive knowing comes about by itself. It is also possible that there is some kind of unconscious or conscious preparation by that person by manner of prayer and meditation. That preparation is a likely spur to bringing the mental faculties to a high pitch, an intensity of intellectual energy. It is possible, I say, because both physically and mentally, it is known that we can be trained and shaped to perform tasks that may have been impossible before.

The two anecdotes of the student and the swimmer are interesting. I do think good vibrations and blessings of evolved souls can help. But if there was a miracle, it was Nature that performed it. When you say the swimmer did not get an appointment, I would not say that is because the Sai Baba knew of that person's eventual death. It is the way some people may explain it to say the fact of death was known. I do not think anybody knows about these things.

The gurus and astrologers do not know about their own deaths. I have come across an instance of a highly popular astrologer who used to charge 5000 rupees to answer a single question about the future. A friend's father was in intensive care after a stroke. The friend went to this astrologer, paid the money and his question was whether his father would pull through. The astrologer gave the definitive reply that the man would recover. After a couple of days, the patient passed away. My friend went back to the astrologer. The answer was that the patient would have lived, but there had been medical negligence. So there it was. As I did say, positivity helps. But in a disease or an accident, there are physical forces, bacteria, body systems, and flesh and bone to contend with too. They work by their own laws.

I do accept the presence of intuition, though it is not always easy to know if your own intuition should be followed in the face of reason and your own understanding of the situation.

Chapter 10 INTUITION AND INNER KNOWING

Bill

Nice. I do agree about the role of Nature ... and the independence of biological laws governing the life and death of our body organs.

Vijay

Bill, we do know that there are certain people with higher levels of sensitivity to emotional and even occult matters. This, of course, includes the medium at a séance attempting to communicate with spirits, but also the people who we say have a *sixth sense* or are clairvoyant and so on. There are tarot readers, *kabala* foretellers and so many others in that line of work. There is a lot of this in the older Eastern cultures. These people are sometimes genuinely gifted with certain perceptions. I would not go to the extent of saying they know. But they have faculties that enable them to make an educated guess. Or, in some very rare cases, they have psychic faculties that enable them to 'see' events that might happen.

Bill

In my childhood, I used to sleepwalk. I remember suddenly waking up at the main gate of my nana's house trying to open the latch when I felt restrained by my uncle, Boba maama, who was holding me back. I had walked down the stairs and through the front courtyard to reach the gate. I must have been around five or six years old at that time. My mum took me to a relative, Lala ji, a saintly person, who would also play sitar at his home. Lala ji was blind from birth. I remember he placed his hand lightly on my head and recited something, which I could not decipher. Later, he brought some ashes from his prayer room and asked my mum to mix it with water, which I was asked to drink. I never sleepwalked again. My mother told me Lala ji was also a good palmist, despite being blind. He would lightly place his index finger on the palm of one's hand and feel the lines. My mum told me all his predictions had come true. How do I explain this?

Another example: as a child, I always feared losing my mum first. Anecdotally, a sadhu had also made a similar prophecy when I was still a toddler: 'This child will first suffer from the death of his mother.' My mum passed on in 2008, after a brief illness. She was sixty-three. I had sensed her death about two years earlier and, accordingly, I had cautioned my dad a number of times, urging him to take good care of her. A few months before she died, I flew suddenly from Perth and got her fully checked at Apollo hospital, Delhi. Nothing sinister was found with her at that time. But she died after a few months. How do I explain my premonition?

I had the same premonition from 1985 to 1989 about the exodus of Kashmiri Bhattas (Pandits) from Kashmir. In fact, four years before the mass exodus, when I met my future wife for the first time in early 1986 in an arranged, facilitated meeting, I asked her if Bhattas would be forced to leave their home one day. She thought for a few seconds and voiced her agreement with me, which proved to be the main reason why I nodded my approval. I was impressed with her *vision* at a time when most Bhattas were still unaware of what was looming. In fact, during 1989 — my last year before my departure from Kashmir towards the end of December — I suffered immensely and warned everyone I knew — at home, at work, and friends and relatives — that our Bhatta community would need to leave home soon. Not many, perhaps none, agreed. They thought I had gone senile, psycho. But history proved me right just a month after I had left.

I have tried to attribute my foretelling of events to my 'sensitive mind', as you have mentioned, and also to my 'natural gift' of deciphering social patterns and the body language of people, with a sharp eye that does not miss much, especially what people say, how, why and when.

Later, in mid-1990, I had a premonition that something sinister was happening in the house of a close relative in Delhi. I warned my closest relative in that family about it and strongly urged her to move out although I had no evidence to support my warning. Luckily, they

Chapter 10 INTUITION AND INNER KNOWING

moved out. Reportedly, a sadistic member of the family had been surreptitiously adding naphthalene balls to their milk, which had adversely affected the nervous system of some members of the extended family. A couple of years later, he was caught red-handed but only after my relatives had moved out.

There are many more examples I can give. I don't know how I get these premonitions; perhaps, due to my sensitivity or the ability to decipher situations. But even I get surprised when I utter warnings out of nowhere about things. It happens spontaneously. My conscious mind is taken by surprise. Perhaps it is my subconscious that processes all the data gathered by my 'five senses', without interacting with my conscious mind. Our conscious mind is a slave to our intellect and ego.

Vijay
Wonderful stuff, very interesting!

Bill
My family moved out of our ancestral house at Alikadal, located in downtown Srinagar, in the early eighties. Since then, I have never visited that house; I have neither had the curiosity nor any nostalgia to go there. But about five years ago, in a dream, I saw the current owners of the house had constructed several windows in a west-facing wall on the fourth storey, which was blind and windowless during my childhood. I called my dad, who confirmed the creation of the new windows in that wall. Incidentally, he had visited that house a few months ago, out of nostalgic yearning. How do we explain my dream?

Coming to dreams, about four years ago, in a daydream (in Perth) I discovered and interacted with a fourteenth-century Muslim saint in Kashmir, Bulbul Shah, who looked extremely angry at a mob protesting outside his *dargah*. He towered above me — about ten feet tall or more — with blood-red eyes. In my dream, he muttered angry words at the local Kashmiri people, who were shouting slogans in a procession. Interestingly, in 1339 CE, Bulbul Shah had played a role in the conversion (to Islam) of Rinchin Shah, who then became the first Muslim king of Kashmir. Please note that, before the dream, I had never heard or known about Bulbul Shah. I had to Google him and call my elders to know more about him.

Again, a few months later, in a daydream (in Perth) I happened to visit the *dargah* of Zeeshan Sahib in Kashmir. I had heard about him but I had never visited his shrine. Over the phone, I described my dream to my aunt, who lives in Kashmir, and described how I reached the *dargah*, the topography of the shrine (located on a hilly slope) and what I saw inside. My description matched the reality.

About two years ago, my father had a dream, when he was in Perth, about a debilitating boil on the back of his elder sister. He called her and described the exact location of the boil. To his surprise, she confirmed she did indeed have a large, painful boil at the same spot on her back. How do we explain it? Love or attachment with a sibling or a loved one? Genetic attachment or subconscious attachment? What is it?

My great-grandfather, a devotee of Goddess Kali, had predicted his death a few hours before he died. Anecdotally, it all happened a day before the wedding of his daughters. He was reportedly hale and hearty, but on that day, after he came out from his prayer (meditation) room, he sat down, called everyone and announced that he was departing soon as he had 'made a blunder'.

Very recently, a friend of mine was rushed to a Perth hospital after suddenly experiencing a cardiac issue. At the hospital, within minutes of his entry directly into the operating theatre, he received two stents. A major artery was almost blocked. He goes to the gym and is fit otherwise. At the hospital, he said to me: 'For some unknown reason, for the last two weeks, after my return from work, I had been asking my wife every day about the symptoms of a heart attack. I had some premonition that something was coming although I was feeling absolutely fit and fine. One must trust one's inner knowing.'

Chapter 10 INTUITION AND INNER KNOWING

Vijay

I have in all my years come across just a few such people who could see in advance of an event. Though there are many who have tried to pretend, for commercial reasons, that they can foretell the future, I think the moment it becomes a business, it loses credibility.

I have come across one such really gifted clairvoyant, Dorothy Rozario Da Cunha, a Goan, who was an extraordinary Christian woman, about sixty years old or so at that time. She was introduced to me at a Christmas party. She was quite well known to the group for her gift of being able to see things in the future. Dorothy had been a school teacher. Some of us at the party were encouraged to consult her and so I did. I was most impressed by what she told me just by holding my hand and looking at me.

I met her a number of times after that; she was a jovial and very compassionate person. Some of her predictions and statements were uncanny in their accuracy. What she told me after a few meetings was, I think, of great portent.

I did get around to asking her about this 'gift'. Such was her kindness that she replied in all seriousness: 'I have been a school teacher all my life and have spent my working years with children. Many years ago, I discovered that I could just sit down and look at the person and somehow I would get to know about that person's nature and life events. It just came naturally to me and no effort was involved, excepting that I had to be still, probably with just the person, and concentrate with my eyes closed, nothing else.'

I then asked her if she performed any special prayer or something. 'Well,' she said, 'I have come from a family that was very religious and going to church and praying was ingrained in us since childhood. But, no, I did not make any special effort to be able to do this. I have often thought about it of course.'

She added, 'There is something that I can tell you. It is this: that we lived very simple lives in my home village in Goa — family, friends, festivals and a sense of wellbeing. I never got married for one reason or another and have lived alone, though quite content and happy.

'The mind is like a slate, a blackboard. When there is too much noise and clutter, too much activity and running about, all of that is like the scribbles I used to make on the blackboard. Sometimes, the children of my class used to take up the chalk and write all over the blackboard, making funny faces and all, or do other things. It is all noise and if all that is in the mind, there is no place for anything else.

'That is the way I see it. When the mind is still and silent, when there is no noise, then it is right on the blackboard by itself.'

Dorothy smiled and certainly, as she said all this, she seemed to know that I understood her and was very happy. 'That is one way of trying to explain it,' she said. 'But in reality, it is God's work. I think He wanted me to help people and that is what I do.'

I have thought often about what Dorothy said to me many years ago. There are no explanations. Just as there are no explanations for so many other mysteries that we live with all around us and don't even notice.

Bill
Beautiful! What Dorothy has said to you is in tune with my thoughts. When the mind is still, without clutter or noise, the subconscious comes into action and takes over — spontaneously — without the conscious level even realising it.

My explanation is that, in such a settled and centralised state of mind, perhaps the subconscious, which is not a slave to intellect or ego, may be connecting with the super-consciousness, which contains all knowledge — from the past, the present and the future. In Hindu thought, we may say when the *Atma* (the soul, consciousness) connects with the *Paramatma* (the super-consciousness), information may be transferred into the conscious level via the subconscious level.

In so far as the foretelling aspect is concerned, my theory is that

Chapter 10 INTUITION AND INNER KNOWING

— as many people have believed in the past and still do believe in the present — it may have all happened before. We may actually be living in the past, as many people believe. People have tried to use the available scientific logic to support their argument. We know when we see a certain star, the rays of light that reach us may have been emitted from that star many, many years ago.

In Kashmir, there have been a number of charismatic saints who would make predictions in very strange and bizarre manners. One such phenomenon was Swami Nand Lal ji, commonly known as Nand-mout. The Kashmiri word 'mout' means 'mad, crazy, lunatic'. Anecdotally, Nand-mout would make unexpected personal and political predictions in very bizarre ways, including predictions about the sudden change in the government, imprisonment for a political leader, and war at the border.

Another such saint was Baghwan Gopinath ji, of whom India issued a postage stamp in the nineties many years after his death. Anecdotally, he had never left his home in his adult life but many people argued, all with strong conviction, that they had sighted him at many places of pilgrimage, interestingly at the same time and on the same day. He was even sighted on the Indo-China border during the 1962 Sino-India war, and during the 1999 Indo-Pak Kargil war, directing the Indian troops to follow a certain route to scale some difficult mountains and elude the trespassers.

These saints have always intrigued me — their predictions and the concurrent sightings of them during their lifetime and long after their death. The only explanation I can come up is perhaps this all has already happened and we are actually living in the past. When people allow their subconscious to connect with the super-consciousness — *without the knowledge and interference of intellect and ego* — they may be able to read the future, which may have already happened. So, such people who may be open-minded and not intellectually extraordinarily brilliant or corrupted or sceptical may possess a mind that is naturally calm, or becomes calm — naturally or by meditation or through religious rituals — which catches the invisible and the unseen, just like a smartphone catches invisible waves and deciphers the information received. The natural sensitivity of a mind may be a major factor in knowing or reading the invisible.

Vijay
It is quite fascinating to read the accounts of your own experiences in this area. Each one of the anecdotes you have recalled here only increased my conviction that there are things which we may perhaps never know. In spite of all the science and the research and the great minds that have been involved in studying these occurrences, we may never really understand, let alone be able to control such gifts by will. Psychologists, neuroscientists and researchers in related fields have been working on these matter and will continue to do so. There may even be theories that try to give explanations as to how it happens and what takes place in the subconscious. But that is about all.

I have found that there has been a tremendous amount of interest in dreaming and the nature of reality among the ancient Greeks as well as the Hindu philosophers. The Buddhist thinkers and teachers have also studied dreams and the subconscious. So I can say that, from the lucidity and detail that you seem to have experienced in your dreams, you are in good company.

Socrates, Plato and Aristotle have all tried to understand and interpret dreams. The first mention of lucid dreaming was made as far back as around 1000 BCE in the Upanishads and also in the Vigyano Bhairav Tantra. We learn from *The Tibetan Book of the Dead* that Tibetan Buddhist monks devoted much of their time to the study of dreams because they thought that lucid dreaming was part of the reality and experience of our lives.

There have been ancient traditions of scholars and erudite men in the courts of kings who were dream interpreters. Much of their work, of course, was unscientific and based on myth and fantasy. Not surprisingly, in the pilgrimage towns of India, such as Haridwar, Rishikesh and Varanasi, there are still pundits and scholars who specialise in the interpretation of dreams.

What is important to us here in our discussion, of course, is whether dreams — like intuition, premonition and visions — are also some kind of messages that come to us. Most of us do not understand them. There are scientific works on the study and interpretation of dreams. I can, at best, say that they are interesting and of value only to the extent that they are efforts to understand what has baffled us for centuries and still does.

The kind of lucid dreams that you have experienced, as with the intuitions you have recounted, underline the fact that these messages from another dimension must not be ignored and should, at the very least, be investigated. Thankfully, science now accepts that these are experiences worth studying and that there are ways in which information is transmitted to us, even though it is not fully understood.

I use the word 'transmitted' quite intentionally as it is my personal belief that our minds are at all times receiving signals and messages from the Great Intelligence that pervades the world. There is intelligence everywhere around us, from the most infinitesimal single-cell organism, the seed and the embryo, to plants, water, animals and humans.

Wherever there is life, there is also intelligence. And with intelligence, there is also communication. Everything communicates and sends messages. I think sometimes we are enabled to receive some messages and sometimes they are so clear that we can decipher them.

Bill
Intuition or premonition of some situations may be due to the wisdom gained from past experience and the intellectual ability to extrapolate to predict future events. As for predicting the future of individuals,

such as by a clairvoyant like Dorothy or by those mystical saints of Kashmir, we really don't know. I have tried to provide some explanation based on my personal understanding of mind but who knows? We may never know!

Vijay
Let me take you, Bill, to our own elders and ancestors in our families and even before them to the Indigenous peoples in many parts of the world. We tend to forget their wisdom and capabilities in the glitter of our new world and our scientific discoveries. All of them were people who belonged to the old folk traditions and to mythologies created by minds that were in constant communication with Nature and with the essential processes of life. I think of them as I sometimes turn away from this crowd of information and data that we sometimes mistake for knowledge. They had none of this. But what they had was the patience to bear witness to life and Nature and to understand their own lives in relation to the world.

I can hardly ever forget a passage from Herman Hesse's novel *Siddhartha*, in which the young Siddhartha is asked by the rich merchant as to what he can do. And Siddhartha answers: 'I can think. I can wait. I can fast.' In those few words, we learn of the lives of our elders and the old peoples who had learnt to live in sustainable harmony with the world that was given to them. What they knew was what they learned from their wonder as they looked up at the stars and thought there were gods and luminous beings in them. They learnt from the seasons and from hearing the sounds of the rain and the storms. The trees spoke to them in the silences of the forests and they began to understand the seasons of the Earth and the seasons of their own lives.

In their patience, they heard all the messages that come to people who have opened their hearts and their consciousness to the mystery that lives. These Indigenous peoples and our elders back in time had the capability, which still survives today in many people who are reflective and sensitive to their environment, of an inner knowing. They could receive the messages that we have spoken of here. They are messages from dimensions that we are not fully aware of, but which are everywhere. The ancients as well as our scientists of quantum physics tell us that vibrations of a cosmic music and sound were the first elements of Creation and of life.

There are some things that we can learn from our ancestors just as there are many things that we have today of great value. We have much knowledge that was not accessible to them. We are also fortunate that we can think of what they had, the knowledge and the wisdom of Nature, and we can learn to get to it.

Bill
So you have taken us back to the Romantic period of Rousseau and Wordsworth, and more recently by Mehjoor, the poet laureate of Kashmir.

Yes, Nature reaches and refines the mind. Nature opens our mind to all possibilities — unbound as is Nature itself. Can we say Nature is the source of all information, from all times? Can we agree Nature is the bank of information and knowledge that some open-minded individuals are able to connect with? Is Nature, therefore, the source of inner knowing? As Dorothy says, God (Nature) nurtures and provides all, including knowledge.

Chapter 11

REALISTIC IDEALISM

Too many ideals get in the way of living practically

There has always been a conflict between the viewpoints of Idealism and Realism. Religion and philosophy have given to the world an idealistic view of life. But the world has aged in time and experience. It is time to take a look again at how best to encounter the times and the world we live in.

In this discussion, we employ the words Idealism and Realism in their common usage meanings: Idealism being the ultimate, utopian and ideal state of things and Realism being things as they are in materialistic life.

Vijay
I am very critical of pure Idealism and push for stark Realism in life. Face it all and don't run away. I think I would like to speak for a pragmatic or a realistic way of living of high values, or perhaps for what is an oxymoron — a *practical idealism*, or a *realistic idealism*.

We are then discussing what might appear to be contradictory. But it can only be said the world has changed so much that both Idealism and Realism, supposed opposites, seem to have a place in redefining each other. In any case, it is also true that in an increasingly free-thinking world, the boundaries between ideas and systems have gotten blurred. I believe this is because we are less rigid in attitudes and are willing to accept good ideas from anywhere. Perhaps that is the essence of liberalism.

I might well warn you, Bill, that I am one of those who believe that pure Idealism has had its day.

Bill

A realistic idealism, I love this topic. The very rigid pursuit of Idealism is seen to kill happiness and the very quality of life. Many unfortunate souls lose sight of the stark reality of life and human nature. They fail to notice the infinite shades of intrinsic imperfection in almost all elements of Nature. So if Nature is not deemed perfect, how do we expect humans to be perfect? Simply oxymoronic, as you say, the theory of realistic idealism! Even our deities are not seen to be perfect although people of devoted belief come up with clever, albeit questionable, theories to justify their imperfection. God can't be imperfect, so they believe.

Vijay

You seem to have gone to the core of the challenge of Idealism: how to get over the unhappiness with reality by creating an ideal. I call it a mental mirage. Harsh words, perhaps, for the dream of perfection that has sustained Idealism for centuries. But then, we must not cringe from being frank even if it is harsh.

My own introduction to Idealism, as perhaps for most people, started with the fancies and extreme goodness of religion served up to me as a youngster. It was beautiful, of course, as the metaphysical Idealism of religious mythology and miracles were wonderful. Though brought up as a Hindu, my parents encouraged the influences of other religions and their fascinating, ennobling human and moral Idealism.

I was exposed to and enjoyed many cultures in the modernising secular India of the latter half of the last century, which was why there was such a cultural shock when I took my first tentative steps into adulthood. Suddenly, I was to be face to face with the real world: imperfect, even ugly. I understood quickly enough that humans are not born or live equal, that good does not usually triumph over evil, and that, at least here on terra firma, the meek do not inherit the Earth. That and many other hard lessons of the realities of life, the hurtful limitations people face, and the compromises that must be made convinced me that religious and moral Idealism was nice but did not really work.

And so, from the days of my callow youth in a world of struggle, began a theme of accepting reality with one's inner nobility of thought, Idealism, if you please, staying intact. It meant, in other words, to keep your eyes wide open to the good, bad and ugly, and also at the same time to deal with it, and do one's bit to change it (as a crusading journalist). Idealism, I began to feel, was needed in certain ways, but not as fantasy or an escape. At best, it was a touchstone, a reference point, to check on reality and to assess what it was and how much better it could be.

Bill
Vijay, perhaps my personal struggles through my life journey mirror yours, but on the subconscious level, as I never thought about many things on the conscious level. The simple reason was that my virgin mind as a child was incapable of thinking, it was mostly instinctive. Most of my responses or reactions, as the case would be, were instant — decided by my subconscious. Why? I don't know. For example, when I was about three years old, I happened to make a connection between a piece of roasted lamb offered to me to eat on an earthen plate and a sheep's skinned body earlier seen hanging in a butcher shop. I instinctively rejected what was offered to me to eat and kicked the earthen plate away, without thinking. Did I know anything about the good or the bad at that age? No. Did I know the poor sheep had been slaughtered, as sacrifice to a deity, and used for human consumption? No. What did I know about humane ethics? Zilch, nothing!

Chapter 11 REALISTIC IDEALISM

My instinctive nature has remained with me through my life. Never have I had to refer to any textbook or religious scripture or elder person for guidance about what is right or what is wrong. My decisions — about the good or the bad —have seldom been based on my thinking. My spontaneous reactions or responses are almost instinctive, right from my subconscious. Perhaps this is the reason I have been called a 'sensitive' person by my elders.

Now, why am I sharing this personal inner side of mine? The reason is I believe I have been a misfit in the most mundane situations of life — at all stages of my life — in most aspects (social, family) and, as a consequence, I have suffered immensely, been bruised and battered mentally. I have had to undergo several levels of enculturation and wear several skins to protect my sensitive mind. Indirectly, my being covered my subconscious with several levels of defensive ego, as a deer (*mrigya*) is protected by its skin (*mrigyashala*).

At this stage, possibly you may be wondering about the absurdity of my story. So let me clarify a little more. Instinctively, my being yearned for an ideal world — loving, nonviolent, honest, fair, empathetic. All this was reflected in my feelings and emotions, and my expectations of the world. I turned vegetarian at about three. Just reiterating, it was all in my nature: instinctive, without enculturation or reference to guiding scriptures. However, as I grew, I discovered the real world was a little different than I was made to believe from those idealistic fairytales and mythological stories. I came across a range of human behaviours that completely stunned and puzzled me. I thought I was from another world. Much human behaviour that is the norm has been alien to me. Even at this stage of my current life, I have not been able to fathom why there are so many religions in the world and why humans fight, kill and rape one another in the name of the religion and also without any religious justification (in the name of nothing).

I have come across some people who relate to my feelings a little and many whose behaviour has hurt me. I may think of the first group as wise, sensitive people, and the latter group as selfish, hedonic or insensitive people. From the former group, I learnt how to deal with the latter group. But learning was not easy. I had to grow layers of skin to become thick skinned. I had to protect myself. This sums up my journey from an idealist mind, which functioned almost instinctively, to a more practical, realistic mind, which takes some time to think and process about a human behaviour or a situation before responding or reacting. But my core has remained unchanged.

I would say it is better to be aware — naturally, as I have been, or through enculturation — about ideals, as reference points, as you have said, and deal with the reality.

Vijay
Your deeply moving study of your own journey to your present self is most interesting in the context. What it tells us is that we are almost all idealistic in our innocence. Unfortunately, most of us are to shed that innocence as we encounter the real world. Most, but not all! Some, I think, develop a useful faculty of becoming realistic but of being able to go back at will to the old Idealism of those days of innocence.

Is it then to be said that the way of Idealism is only valid in our childhood and early youth? Is it as inevitable as growing older, that we also turn cynical and lose the sensitivity that you speak of? No. The answer that comes to me is a big NO.

The sensible and sensitive person learns and transforms in behaviour and responses to be able to live. He or she is always self-aware and knows the transformation is needed. But there is now wisdom in place of withdrawal and vulnerable sensitivity. To put it simply, it is best to never go too far away from yourself. As you transform, with full awareness of how you yourself are reshaping your clay, you also reshape your Idealism.

All through our lives we go through an inner conflict. You see, we are always exposed to *religious idealism, romantic idealism, moral* and

Chapter 11 REALISTIC IDEALISM

patriotic idealism and so on. There are always hard, sometimes challenging, realities and there are situations that we are programmed not to face.

As you can see, we are not denying or getting away entirely from Idealism. I don't think we can because it is a natural yearning of humans to seek the highest and the best — to seek even the transcendental even if it is never to be achieved. Essentially, we are talking about, exploring, the possibility of transforming our vision of the Ideal to suit us in life in the world.

I have already touched upon religious idealism — gods with supreme powers and supreme goodness, just retribution for good or evil deeds, and a perfect, moral world. That is the Ideal. If it is not found here, say the religions, you will get it in the hereafter. I have two problems with that. I am not willing to wait for the hereafter. It is too iffy. Secondly, the goodness demanded is much too rigid, much too self-torturous. They deny too much of the joy of living. In fact, that denial of some natural and quite harmless pleasures is a problem too. When very high ideals are set, people, mere mortals, adore them, keep them high on a pedestal. And forget about them. The business of real life takes over.

Most often, the ideals are there like totems. Just knowing they have ideals is quite enough for people. They become hypocrites, idealistic humbugs. In fact, they say the ideals are great but too difficult and so let us get on with the sin and evil that is needed. We can always offer confession to a priest, or gold jewellery and idols to a temple, and so on, to ask forgiveness, which is why it is a fact that religious organisations are some of the richest in the world. The dropout idealists are making deals with their gods.

There was a time I read a lot of the writings of philosopher president Dr Sarvepalli Radhakrishnan. I still have his two volumes on Indian philosophy on my desk. Capital stuff, a tremendous scholar. It was his view, repeated often, that this was 'an ethical universe'. If you read more, he seemed to suggest that if the ideals of religion were followed, then there was complete order and justice, everything was in its place, and so on. As a questioning person, I was astounded by his idealistic blindfold. Hey, I asked, what happened to the misery heaped on good, innocent people, the power and wealth that goes to evil-doers, the inhumanity of high and low castes? What happened to all the suffering of humankind? The idealist view of life just ignores reality.

It was then that I began to be convinced that much of the pure Idealism is not only just philosophy, but also about 'us and them'. A very few people — the rich, the privileged and the educated — can be idealistic while the rest have to just lump it with hard reality. For those poor and underprivileged, the Idealism of religion and of politics too is just a sedative, the 'opiate of the masses'.

An opiate or a psychedelic fix is what pure Idealism becomes. Because, unless we bring our own understanding and wisdom of experience into living, we cannot make sense of the realities we must live with.

Bill

Vijay, I agree with you about the reshaping of clay as we grow older, which means the clay remains the same but gets remoulded with age and takes a more practical shape that can deal with the attrition of the real world.

I also agree that only some, or perhaps none at all, retain their sensitivity and innocence with age. How do they do it? Perhaps they learn to deal with it, perhaps they learn to wear a thicker skin at times of crises, personal or impersonal — an additional skin that they can remove at will in order to return to their natural, sensitive self.

I believe the degree of our empathy, care, passion and love — as interpreted and understood in common usage — is directly proportional to the degree of our sensitivity which, in turn, is inversely proportional (in a more scientific language) with the degree of ego and the layers of ego we develop in our growing years due to our circumstances and the hardships we suffer in our early years.

Chapter 11 REALISTIC IDEALISM

There are times I have cried as an adult — I still do — when my sensitivity and innocence is challenged. But I have learnt to deal with it based on the wisdom of experiences I have accumulated as an adult. I may not have changed much at my inner core but I have acquired the skills to deal with my sensitivity, which I have discovered is my real and perhaps only gift from Nature. My rare gift qualifies me to be more humane and empathetic.

Vijay
No, there is no skin and there is no addition of a mask to what I am. I have lived through struggle and moderate success but those materially successful people of ego and their world was never my world. I was with them because I had to be and earn money. So it was done. But the world I did not want, of greed and ugliness and dirty competition, was never my world. I saw it all from a distance. So I never really lost the innocence of childhood and perhaps also the vulnerability that is part of being sensitive. I think this should answer your question.

I became an editor and had big teams and parties and all that and was a leader and it was fun. But I was doing it. Doing it and not living it. What I was living was what I am, with my thinking and trying to understand things and writing stuff, also reading stuff from your book, which I started yesterday.

So there it is. All children regardless of their circumstances are affectionate. They can sense love and kindness. I like that.

Bill
Religious idealism, as you call it, was perhaps necessary to create some sort of discipline in society, some kind of order, which would implicitly and explicitly exhort and urge people, right from their early childhood, to strive for some kind of perfection, seen now as Idealism. As described, illustrated and defined in the religious texts, people had the moral and ethical behaviours of many so-called noble, brave and

just people to emulate. For example, Shri Ram has been perceived and promoted as *Purshottam*, a man of the highest order or the most perfect man.

We must keep in mind that the definitions of the qualifying terms — such as good, bad, noble, brave and just — have been changing over time and are also subject to the practical causes and needs of a community, which keep changing.

Gandhi, who is revered around the world as he was in India in the twentieth century, is now made to look like a person of weak character, blamed for the division of India and seen in a poor light. Many Indians now feel they don't need a Gandhi or his ideals at present. They believe they need someone exactly the opposite of Gandhi to lead them to achieve the so-called past glory of India.

In the past century, democracy was seen as a just and humane system of governance, but no longer. Idealistic views have changed over time.

Why is this happening? I think it is borne out of human material greed and competition, which have been exacerbated by high population growth. As I have always maintained, the human understanding and practice of Idealism has been subject to our struggles and our needs in a more practical world, which have significantly been affected by population growth. Note that the human race has multiplied itself nearly eight times in the past four centuries. Our struggles have also multiplied accordingly.

As you say, the rich and the educated may, in theory, have a more idealistic view of the world and of life in general, but the predominant poorer section of society has to deal with the real world, as it comes, and has no time to strive for an ideal life.

For them, it is a matter of survival — by hook or by crook — and not the pursuit of Idealism. They have model figures like Shri Ram or Shri Krishna before them to follow but that is only through their religious pursuit, through prayers and rituals. Even they know they can never emulate these deities. They practically use their deities for material favours and don't follow them.

How many followers of Sai Baba practically follow his austere life and the core message, 'God is one! Be patient and have faith'? For them, he is a giver of wealth and every other material gift. They drape his idol in silk and gold, as a bribe, even though in reality he was a holy man who lived with the poor and lived like them in poverty. He was a renunciate who owned nothing. Now his statue and seat are gilded and offerings of gold are made.

Vijay
There is something else, Bill. It was men who controlled religions and we see that the men heaped all of their Idealism on women. It became a weapon of male chauvinistic subjugation of women. Goodness and sacredness is often used as a weapon. That is the height of human ingenuity: to be able to use even Idealism as a weapon.

That's nothing new. All our conquerors and religious crusaders justified their barbarism of forcing wars on other people by proclaiming, and also believing, that their ideal religion and only their ideal God was good for those other people. Let us not forget that Hitler and the Nazis had ideals of a master race and a supreme Germany and would destroy most of the world for that.

Idealism without liberal humanism is always dangerous and cruel. You see, Idealism is lofty and larger than life and that is why it is so attractive to us. Humankind is forever trying to overreach itself. We are always trying to be more than what we are. This certainly brings progress in every sphere. But it also brings mad ambition and megalomania.

You spoke about Gandhi. Yes, the quintessential idealist that he was in his ideas, it is interesting to see that he also gave them a practical shape. The ideal of nonviolence made all kinds of sense at that time in India in the political circumstances. India could never fight or dislodge the British by violence or any other means. His nonviolent resistance was shaped very practically and cleverly to mobilise and motivate the masses. Take a small example. He led a march of people to the seashore to get seawater to make salt from. An innocuous act but since salt concerns everybody, and had a British tax on it that was flouted by this mass salt making, it became a big revolutionary act.

Gandhi went on to make nonviolence a universal and infallible creed to be applied in every situation. It could never work. It doesn't always work even in personal life if you or your loved ones are attacked. It can never work if you face a terrorist or if a nation faces an army. In such situations, you have to say goodbye to Idealism and face reality with a realistic response.

It is the real world that demands realistic action from you. That is mainly the reason why Gandhi, though he has the respect and adulation he deserves, is also irrelevant in many world situations today.

The world has changed. As you point out, the world population is many times what it was a mere four centuries ago. So the demands on natural resources are increased and there is more competition. Other things have happened. There is greater awareness of gender and racial inequality. More people, millions more people, want more.

How we think of ideals and, on the other hand, how we manage to be practical is also something that is to be worked out anew by each one of us and our societies and nations. Very simply, we are all being forced to be more realistic.

An ugly side-effect

I have already said that ideals that are too lofty and difficult to practise or achieve tend to put people off. It also happens that the assertion of too many such ideals causes tension and conflict. This pertains especially to social behaviour and morality. Let me work with some examples. Most religions and societies have heaps of ideals of behaviour, chastity and modesty only for women. These are ideals fashioned by men because it was largely men that created religions.

We know about the ideals of chastity and the chastity belts in medieval England and Europe. In India it was worse as the ideal of chastity and honour of women demanded that if their husbands were killed in battle, the wives would commit self-immolation by walking into a burning funeral pyre. It is sometimes argued that this custom, terrifying to say the least, came about to save the women from slavery and rape. Perhaps, and perhaps not!

The custom of women committing self-immolation, or sati, went on to be followed in times of peace as well in many parts of India. Women of high station and honour were supposed to do it to preserve the ideal of chaste Indian womanhood. Once the lady of a royal or noble position was burnt alive on the pyre of her husband, she was given the lofty status of 'Sati Mata' or a goddess, and was worshipped in a small, specially erected temple. Nobody asked the women of course. It was an ideal.

There are numerous examples of these ideals of behaviour pertaining to women. In the Islamic tradition, it is thought that women must hide their faces and bodies behind a burqa or hijab so they cannot divert and tempt men from the ideals of abstinence and restraint. Even in the secular west, men are also thought to not be able to control their own behaviour and are provoked by the way a woman dresses, reflecting universality of men.

There are so many of these ideals of social behaviour. The big one is, of course, the Indian ideal of human evolution and purity of blood lines that took shape in the odious and unjust custom of caste. The high-born were the Brahmins (to be scholars and teachers and priests), followed by the Kshatriyas (warriors and rulers) and the rest were condemned to permanent subordination. This was a vision, in a time of the decline of Hinduism, of an ideal society. The caste demon is still alive and well. The *untouchables* – called the *Dalits* – are not meant to mingle with people from the upper four castes of Hindus.

I think goals and ideals should be a matter of individual choice and be compatible with one's nature. When they are forced on a group or society, they become a form of coercion and injustice.

Nobody is perfect and nobody leads an ideal life. We have seen many godmen, monks and priests, who are supposed to follow strict rules of sexual abstinence and chastity, being involved in ugly cases of rape and molestation.

More human-friendly ideals would be definitely more realistic.

Bill

You have now raised women and caste issues. Are you trying to imply that Idealism has been driven mainly by men — strong men in high places — who use it to empower themselves by thrusting it on the physically weaker (women) and underprivileged (lower castes)?

The Hindu ritual of *sati*, child marriages, widows shaving their heads and women covering their heads and faces are some of the most egregious examples of Idealism being enforced by men on women.

Even Mata Sita was asked to take the fire test (*agnipariksha*) after Lankan King Ravana was defeated and killed. As if that was not enough, she was abandoned by her husband, Shri Ram, after a common citizen refused to follow Shri Ram's example and did not accept his own wife who had spent some time away from him. Why are all tests to be taken by women? Why is it only women that have to be perfect — in looks, intelligence and character?

How about men? For their part, how many Hindu men follow Shri Ram in his ideal life? How many men are punished for adultery?

In India, parents expect high levels of self-discipline, character and restraint from their daughters, but not their sons. Ideals are thrust on daughters but sons generally get away from them. Often it is their own mothers, instead of fathers, who give them more freedom. Where fathers are strict disciplinarians of their sons, mothers may undermine that discipline (and the father's authority) by consciously

Chapter 11 REALISTIC IDEALISM

or inadvertently pampering and spoiling their sons. This scenario may, particularly, reflect the case of mothers who pamper their sons in the Indian and similar patriarchal cultures where male children are generally preferred over females. There can be different reasons of this behaviour. Possibly, mothers see their sons as their physical shields against their own oppressive husbands or in-laws or the community in large. Possibly, also due to the dowry issue in such cultures and that boys carry on the name of the dynasty whereas girls leave home and become a part of some other family. In such systems, the status of the boy's family is seen as higher than the girl's family. Female foeticide is seen in many parts of India. I have written quite a bit about this issue is my earlier books, *Issues White-anting India* (2017) and *A Bouquet of Random Thoughts* (2019). Such cultures need a total shift in the social paradigm to address the issue sooner than later.

In conclusion, I think the concept of Idealism has been wielded mainly on the weak and poor. All rules — social, religious and political — apply to mainly the weak and the poor. Others usually get out of it and are even permitted to. Where the poor and the weak fight against those concepts of Idealism, in their own minds or explicitly in the real world, they suffer immensely through personal guilt or through repercussions in the world.

In the end, if one is allowed to think rationally, with an open mind, and allowed to analyse a deity or a god without facing socio-religious repercussions, one can easily discover there is no ideal god or a good-only god. All deities and gods have been shown to have shortcomings, similar to the humans who created them.

Human imperfections are clearly reflected in their creations, their gods. If Nature is not really perfect or ideal, how do we humans expect to be perfect? Idealism is a myth. The only pragmatic solution, to capture the essence of Idealism and yet be practical, is to adopt an approach of realistic idealism, as you wisely suggest. Realistic idealism seems to be the way forward.

Vijay

Using ideals against the subjugated or the poor has always been done as a mechanism of control. A simple example from all world histories is that the ruling classes and kings and nobles were never bound by ordinary social morality. They could be complete hedonists, flouting every rule of behaviour, with as many wives or mistresses as they wanted, and killing when they wanted or whom they wanted. There were no rules for them. This, not surprisingly, is true even today of the very rich and powerful. Though now with the media always around, they are a bit more careful. Even so, the immoralities of the rich and famous are admired and read about. If a middle-class or poor person did the same things, they would be condemned.

Clearly, ideals are different and selective for different people, which is why, in today's world of free thought and free speech, people question ideals.

I must share with you here an interesting observation by an ordinary tea-stall owner who I thought was rather wise. He had a tea stall near a film studio in Mumbai and had watched at least three generations of film stars around the film studio. He spoke to me about the moralities and characters of people.

'Only the middle-class people are afraid of moral rules and of what will people say. So they are very moralistic, or try to be. The very rich and the very poor don't care. Look at the world around you as I have seen it sitting here. The big guns don't give a damn. And I see in the fishing village where I live, that those working people don't give a hoot for morals. It is only the middle class.'

Well, there were echoes in what he said of Shaw's Pygmalion and 'middle-class morality'. But I thought he made sense. The very rich and the poor have no time to follow ideals but keep them like people keep pictures of gods on the wall. The middle class are the only ones that really bother and try to follow ideals. And when they can't, they become hypocrites.

Chapter 11 REALISTIC IDEALISM

I think that all of this really comes down to something we hinted on at the outset: that Idealism has changed too. The world has aged. That is true in terms of the passage of time, human events and experience, and human knowledge. You and I today have more information, access to knowledge and hindsight on history than our ancestors. We may not live in a better world or we may not be wiser. But we know more and have seen more and also have a cynicism that questions fantasy and Idealism.

And so it is that being modern and being liberal and free of mind and speech, we have also become practical in the ways that we live.

We will have ideals of course. New ideals in new situations will come to us, but I feel sure that they will be a bit more realistic; perhaps, instead of looking at the planet Mars as a god, we will now think of how to get there and colonise it.

An interesting conversation about religion

Bill

Looking at the current strife in northeast India, Kashmir and Ayodhya, a well-meaning friend, Ashis Gupta (an engineer by profession) said: 'My view is all religions should be banned with immediate effect. People may practise religion at home but not in public. Only art and culture can be practised or promoted in public or in mass gatherings, like music concerts or ballet or theatre. Religious places should be converted into museums — the important ones with history or architecture. The rest should be demolished to make schools or hospitals or parks, and sports places of course.'

I said to him he had an idealist view and added: 'I agree in principle. But that is an idealistic socialist cum communist thought. That is what happened in the Soviet Republic and remains so in China. In India, however, you so will meet strong resistance from Hindutva and other religious groups.'

He replied, 'I am talking about change worldwide, and not merely in India.'

I cautioned him: 'It won't happen. It is impractically idealist. Religion is used for reaping geopolitical, socio-economic and commercial dividends. It has become a necessity. Imagine Saudi Arabia without Islam. Imagine Europe without Christianity. Imagine Thailand and Sri Lanka sans Buddhism, and India without Hinduism. Religion is in the very fabric of life and ethos. Businesses run because of it. Famous centres of pilgrimage — the Tirupati, Shirdi and Vaishnav Devi shrines — are run as proper businesses. People's faith is cashed in on.'

And he responded: 'The human race was not created with religion. Religion is something humans invented to protect themselves and each other. Faith was needed to survive through hardship. Religion has outlived itself and become an unnecessary evil. Imagination is a powerful tool ingrained in humans. You have to imagine something strongly and collectively to make it happen tomorrow or someday. Look at what science has achieved today. Who would have imagined one hundred years ago the world of today?

'But yet some people did, imagine I mean — scientists, thinkers, physicists — and all of those imaginings are realities today. All of those thoughts are realities today. So who knows what tomorrow holds for us? Maybe religion will become history if we wish for it collectively and strongly. But is not human civilisation a journey through experiments, some triumphant, some fruitless and some even catastrophic?'

I concluded: 'Yes, that is the real world. Idealism changes shape and form. In each of its new shapes and forms, it sets up a new benchmark, a new bar, a new standard, a new set of expectations from humans.'

This conversation with this friend, and his reaction, illustrate a classic case of Idealism: a journey from one extreme to another extreme. He is perhaps seeking Idealism in scientism as well as implicitly, or explicitly, in communism and socialism. He is seemingly sick of strife caused by religion. Perhaps he is not sick of religion, as religions by themselves are just harmless thoughts, but he is possibly sick of religious exploitation and the strife caused by the drivers and followers of religions. He is sick of politicians who abuse and misuse religions for their selfish ends or ideological drives.

Vijay
Well, one can classify your friend's ideas in all those 'isms' but I for one would agree with him to a great extent that religion and even Idealism must be personal and for yourself. It must be for the individual to realise and to think about at the highest levels. Societies and nations must have real goals that are human friendly and practical.

Bill
The world is caught in a fight between Realism and Idealism. In the real world, might is right. The big fish eats the smaller fish, by hook or by crook. It is a human jungle, capitalistic and materialistic. Humans are cruel to not only animals but other humans too. In the real world, strife is the perpetual norm, dangling from one extreme to the other. The present world is real but can be deemed unsustainable due to human imprudence, greed, arrogance and misadventure. Its crash is inevitable. In an ideal world, which we humans must collective and proactively strive for, every human should be considered equal and humaneness must prevail over hedonic materialism and the known ill-effects of capitalism. Environmental sustainability of the planet must be ensured and all life forms must be looked after, so that the world is more sustainable and a better place to live for our future generations. Time alone will tell which world will eventually win – the world that we presently live in or the world that we must sincerely strive to create. I hope the latter world prevails. The solution may lie in *realistic idealism*, which will help us to achieve the intended objectives whilst being conscious of the negative sides of humans and devise ways to manage them effectively, through holistic education.

Idealism must conform to Realism otherwise it becomes a punishment for those who practise it. It must adapt to the real world, the actual circumstances and the changing times. Pragmatism, and not Idealism in a strict sense, is more prudent for achieving practical solutions.

Change is the only constant. Idealism changes with Realism. The real world forces it to change. Truth prevails over the imaginary. Realism prevails over Idealism.

Chapter 12

THE TERRIFYING QUESTION

What if the wise ones have got it all wrong?

The religions are sure of themselves and their doctrine. So are the cults and spiritualists. Everybody says they have the answers. But there is a big question: what if they have all got it wrong?

Vijay
There are so many faiths, so many beliefs and so many versions of what is right and what is the true destiny of humankind, of each one of us. Different cultures and civilisations have imagined heavens and hells, and salvation and nirvana, and rebirth and Karma, philosophies and theologies to get to the Truth of the great mystery: why are we here and how must we live? There is so much wisdom on these matters and so many ways for humans to follow.

Bill
Is that not interesting — so many religions, each claiming authenticity and superiority? Using a simplistic mathematical logic, that means all other religions are wrong. Going by that logic, if they all individually claim the sole authenticity and, thereby, implicitly prove all other religions wrong, they all prove one another wrong and, therefore, they all must be wrong. If there was one true religion, there would

be no need for the creation of so many religions and faiths, as there would be no disagreement between people. But that has obviously not happened. Individual disagreements between the proponents of religions has, over time, led to deviations in beliefs, giving birth to new religions, religious sects, subsects and subfaiths. For instance, take the case of Abrahamic religions — Judaism, Christianity and Islam. But it does not stop there. Christianity and Islam each, in turn, gave birth to several sects. Similarly, the Indian subcontinent's religions, from Vedic to Buddhism to Jainism to Sikhism, all also have deviations. The times have forced change and resulted in the creation of new sectarian thoughts.

The most interesting part is, despite the variations, all religions and their sects coexist and thrive at the same time. So many truths, plus all those religions and spiritual gurus have managed to gather their own followers. If you challenge the superiority of any religion or religious sect — and not the religion itself — that would potentially be considered blasphemous and potentially be punishable by mob lynching or by the state law, as inferred, facilitated or expressed.

Vijay
When you talk about so many religions and their sects, you are underscoring the fact that humans can and do create religions at will. Also new religions and sects come along — firstly, as and when newer beliefs are needed and, secondly, when there are other people with ideas who wish to be powerful. In all of that, the real point of religion, which is to find a way to Divinity and a better human life, is obscured. Wealth and power have become an important element for those who control religions. That is doubtless one of the major ways in which we went wrong.

The moment religion became an organised activity, with controllers and gatekeepers who took over as God's middle-men, it became a business enterprise with the products on sale being salvation, conso-

Chapter 12 THE TERRIFYING QUESTION

lation to the miserable and hope to the depressed, the performance of ceremonies and so on. This was inevitable perhaps. But somehow all religions became collectors of vast wealth. It did not matter where the wealth came from. With the wealth and power came dubious materialistic, societal and political involvements.

The many religions that you mention, with their many sects and gods, combine to make a supermarket of Divinity. People can take their pick. There was never any possibility of one religion. Every religion had a localised identity and was created out of events and circumstances in certain geographical areas. At the time these religions came into being, there were hardly any modern modes of communication or travel. So the major religions stayed in their areas with their own versions of God and own beliefs.

Bill

You seem to have hit the nail on its head: religions becoming gradually obscure due to the ever-changing nature of how humans use them, driven by intrinsic greed for power and control over other humans. So you agree humans make and shape their religions based on what they need and when they need it.

I am reminded of Henry VIII, the King of England from 1509 to 1547, who founded the Anglican Church. He is best known for his fallout with the Pope on getting his first marriage (to Catherine of Aragon) annulled, which resulted in his initiating the English Reformation and separating the Church of England from the papal authority. His first wife did not bear him a male heir. So he had an affair with Mary Boleyn, Catherine's lady-in-waiting. But after he found she too was incapable of bearing him any children, his eyes fell upon Mary's younger sister, Anne Boleyn, a charismatic person in the Queen's entourage. When she did not agree to become his mistress, he decided to marry her, for which he needed to divorce Catherine. He appointed himself as the supreme head of the Church of England, as the Anglican

Church is now known, and did what he intended to do. He married six times.

I am also reminded of many gurus who would surround themselves with an administrative inner circle of devotees. One could not meet these gurus without the permission and blessings (through bribe) of those powerful henchmen and henchwomen.

And what would these gurus say? Would they say anything different to the religion they were born into? No. They just created their own style of delivering the same old messages of the past — like pouring old wine in new bottles — but with clout, using excellent performing skills. In a way, these gurus created minor deviations of their religion to exploit people's ignorance, all for material needs. Anecdotally, once inside the sect, one would find it extremely difficult to leave; one would be hounded by the henchmen. It is like the scenario depicted in 'Hotel California', the iconic seventies song by the legendary musical group the Eagles.

Now how do these gurus flourish? The answer is they just feed on inherent human insecurity and fallibility, general ignorance, impatience, greed and the tendency to want shortcuts. Generally, these gurus are street smart and possess good hypnotising skills, with a good understanding of human psychology. For their part, their followers pay for the three I's — insecurity, ignorance and impatience.

Ask any follower of the Sai Baba of Shirdi about his core message. More often than not, the person may not know. Sai's simple message was: 'Our master is one, have faith and impatience'. Although this is one of the greatest messages humans can possibly receive, the Sai followers have successfully created a new sect after him, constructing his temples across the length and breadth of India, draping his idols in silk and gold in every temple. Ironically, most people may beg him for material benefits. How sad Sai's simple message could have alleviated them of lots of suffering in life. His simple, core message is priceless — a panacea for living a good life, especially in a multi-faith country

Chapter 12 THE TERRIFYING QUESTION

like India, which is so multicultural and multi-ethnic, where people have divided themselves based on religions, sects, castes and what not, where these divisions are consciously being strengthened by politicians to divide and rule. Sai's message could unite India but did not, as the powerful and wealthy have all along been proactively nourishing and nurturing the religious and caste divides.

People — like God — are known by many names, both formal and nicknames, by their own parents, siblings, friends, colleagues and strangers, and later by their partners, children and grandchildren. How disappointing to see individuals fighting one another when they are related to each other in some way. How can there be different gods overseeing different religions if the human anatomy is the same in people from all faiths? Simply illogical! Don't all people die in the end? Yes. Does one's religion matter and is it asked at the time of receiving a blood transfusion or medication? No. Why humans are discriminated against based on their religion, caste, colour and gender? Are not such acts of bias and discrimination against our fellow humans, with whom we share 99.9 percent of our DNA, bizarre and blasphemous if the perpetrators believe in God? [Note: Jehovah's Witnesses are a notable exception in terms of refusing blood transfusion and medication.]

Yes, religion is being used as a facility, as a commodity, as a resource to gain wealth and power, as a weapon to subjugate people and control them.

One day, hopefully, humans may wake up from their deep slumber, open their eyes, use their common sense and realise religion itself is harmless — a moral school, like a university — but that politicians and religious leaders have been exploiting it for their own selfish motives.

Vijay
Well Bill, the gurus are a great Indian speciality. I have met and interacted with a few of them and would like to share some impressions here. I met Maharishi Mahesh Yogi of Transcendental Meditation

(TM) fame in the seventies. He was the guru of The Beatles and ran a big organisation. TM was big then. I was a young reporter and got a brief interview with him.

I asked him if TM was taken from the Indian tradition of yoga. He shook his head with an angry wave of his hand. 'No, not at all,' he said, 'it is my own, my own invention. Of course, I am an ambassador of Indian spirituality. But TM is my very own thing.' I found him to be highly intelligent and quick on the uptake. As I interviewed him, what came across was that he had taken yogic and Buddhist meditation techniques and come up with TM. At that time, a few million followers practised TM all over the world. So what you say about the changing needs of people and new faith systems is right on. Though TM was not a new faith, it was a kind of spirituality beyond traditions of faith.

The hugely successful, controversial and couldn't-care-less godman Osho was in Pune when I got an interview with him. He was something else — a mesmerising personality. He had just finished a brief talk to his followers, mostly foreigners, in which he had said: 'God is a joker ...' and some such remarks. I asked him about this. He laughed all the time and explained that all of our lives are a big joke, not to be taken seriously. It was heady stuff, shocking and comic yet serious too. The followers loved him for his breezy spirituality. And again, there were millions of them.

These were two of our most successful gurus. There were others and there are some even now. There are also a lot of charlatans. The really good ones are clever men, spiritual salesmen who know what their audience wants. And so they create alternative mini-religions that are simple, easy and even a lot of fun. They do not question or debunk traditional beliefs and they don't have new gods. I think they have such large followings because people are a bit tired of old, rigid religions. They want to enjoy their spirituality, which, I think, is quite alright.

Chapter 12 THE TERRIFYING QUESTION

Bill

Can't agree more! Yes, that is what some clever opportunistic humans do. They feel the pulse of the world during their times and accordingly shape traditional wisdom, which sells with a relative ease. Bear in mind, they just sell old wines in new bottles and nothing more. They also benefit from a large fanbase who worship and defend them when challenged. Mass mentality is herd mentality. The masses do not think, they follow like a machine, like a herd.

They attack — with anything they have, including social media — anything they deem blasphemous in their eyes. Fear works in favour of these gurus. Fear always works.

What if it was all wrong?

Vijay

It is a ghost of doubt, a primeval terror about us, but it is there. Have we deluded ourselves, taken the wrong direction and made a big, big mistake about religions and gods and the purpose of life — a mistake for all the centuries that we are aware of human worship and gods, perhaps going back about 4000 years?

Life has been here for millions of years. Modern humans evolved nearly 200,000 years ago and we know that by the Neolithic period (starting from about 10,000 BCE), humans had spiritual and religious ideas and lived and thought of life and Nature and creation. Our ancestors at that time were aware, were thinking and trying to understand life and the world, just as we are doing even today. But what was there before that? There is research, of course, and the educated guesses of scientific people who tell us of animistic gods and mother goddess cults and paganism and so on. It is something we will never know, what humans thought of and worshipped, if we did, and what kind of wisdom we had, say, 10,000 years ago.

Among researchers and academics, there has been awareness of the knowledge and wisdom of the ancients. But among ordinary modern people, and this is not surprising, we compare that old wisdom and knowledge with what we know at present. It is a bit like you and me, looking back at our grandparents — who had no computers, internet or mobile phones — and to think that we know more or are wiser than them. My own grandson expresses surprise when I tell him that when I was his age, nearly sixty years ago, we had no television, no computer games and no YouTube, no mobile phones either. We must remember that in the early days of our own elders, and going back thousands of years of humankind, people lived good and complete lives and had intellectual abilities just as we have, so that they could make up their theories and ideas and systems to live well and fully. They did not have heaps of information and media; that was all.

The wisdom of life and living, wisdom about Nature and the cosmos, imagination and the ability to find a deep harmony in Creation, I think these have very little to do with just information and data. Our grandparents knew and thought and philosophised and had a wonderful quality of life too. Science and modern medicine have given us a lot more than what they had, but we still do not have any significantly better world than them. And we can go further and further back to thousands of years and still assume that the ancient human, who had the same brain and mind and body as us, had understood what life was all about in a different way.

There were obviously other ways of living and thinking and knowing life's purpose. What we have now as our existential ideas have evolved from the ancient Greek, Persian, Mayan, Egyptian, Chinese and Indian civilisations of the last 4000 years. And we think what has evolved from there, and what scientific knowledge has been added, is all that can be. We have a familiar and very well-defined ontology of humankind, a sure-fire pattern of our destiny on Earth and in the afterlife. And all social behaviour and morality is fixed. The only thing is that they are fixed in different ways in different civilisations and religious systems,

Chapter 12 THE TERRIFYING QUESTION

all different, some opposed to each other. They can't all be right.

The fact there are so many systems also points to the possibility that there can be many more systems. And also that before the present systems, there were other very different systems. We presume that the only way to live and think is the way we have now. But how do we know this is the best way or that it is the way that Nature and Creation have devised for us?

With the kind of problems that even our best ideas in our religious and spiritual thought have created, also the tremendous conflict and misery caused by our political and social systems, it is clear that at some times and at some places, humankind has gone wrong. Perpetual conflict and perpetual strife could not be our true and only destiny. And since everything that we have created around us comes from the mind and other basic beliefs, it is but natural that we think in terms of changing the ways in which we think and live.

Bill
Vijay, I think before I proceed with my response, I must first get some figures right based on the published literature — about the age of our Earth, the life on the Earth and the age of homo sapiens (modern humans). As per current scientific theories, the age of our Earth is believed to be about 4.54 billion years and the age of life on the Earth is believed to be at least 3.5 billion years. That means life on the Earth did not possibly exist in the first one billion years after the creation of the Earth.

All modern humans are classified as homo sapiens. Interestingly, homo sapiens are believed to be just 300,000 years old, based on the fossils discovered recently. Previously, the age of homo sapiens was believed to be about 200,000 years old. It is now understood that early homo sapiens did not come after the Neanderthals but were their contemporaries. However, it is likely that both modern humans and Neanderthals descended from Homo-Heidelbergensis. This means our species of humans first began to evolve nearly 300,000 years.

In the context of 3.5 billon years of life on the Earth, the human age of 300,000 years is quite negligible in mathematical terms. Now, here are the questions we need to answer:

- Before modern humans, who are just 200,000–300,000 years old, who workshopped God during those first 3.5 billion years of the creation and evolution of life? Which religion was followed, and by whom? The answer to those two questions answers your question. Perhaps, no one and none.
- Before the creation of each religion, were the earlier religions — on the time scale of human creation — wrong? Who decided they were wrong? Who was the authority? Obviously, humans only.
- Were religions created as a necessity — as a reaction to the times humans lived in — and for convenience? Possibly, yes.
- Will more religions be created in the future for convenience, commerce and empowerment over humans? Possibly, yes.

Vijay

When you go back thousands, even a few hundred thousand years in time, it is impossible to even guess what our human ancestors worshipped. Fossils and findings at ancient burial sites have provided some scanty information. Burial ceremonies reveal, for instance, in Europe, that figurines of Venus (as a fertility goddess) were placed in graves. We know of ancient gods in Greek, Nordic, Roman, Egyptian and Indian civilisations. But as there is no evidence of any gods existing before 10,000 BCE, that question may never be answered.

We can only imagine and surmise about the religious aspects of the lives of the ancients. It is fascinating even to sit back and try to imagine what humans — with our kind of brains and feelings and responses to natural events — thought of as the powerful forces that affected their lives.

Chapter 12 THE TERRIFYING QUESTION

The true and deep feeling of consciousness of Divinity is natural in humankind. It is as natural as, and is perhaps a form of, love, devotion, an emotion of transcendence. And that is why, in essence, religion is a personal experience of heart and soul. When it becomes a mass social activity, it begins to lose some of its meaning.

Bill
Well said, Vijay. You rightly speak of the lack or paucity of information about any kind of religion practised by humans 10,000 years ago. Going by general human restlessness and the intrinsic tendency to create something new, there must have been numerous localised practices among the human habitats — unorganised and informal religions. Their understanding of gods and religious practices, which would have been mostly ritualistic — a practice of ritualism rather than spiritualism — would have been dependent upon the volume of proven knowledge they had, their circumstances and the challenges they faced from the elements of Nature, their fears of the unknown — birth, death, disease, natural calamities and so on.

Although there is a dire paucity of information about them and their rituals and religions, perhaps because they did not write them as we do, I believe religions would have always been there in one form or another — ritualistic or spiritualistic or both at the same time. After all, whenever people have fears, they create religions and turn to their God, both an inner god, as a guardian angel of belief, or the one common God.

Let us just look at the religious rituals at times of births, weddings and deaths. These rituals cost money. People in the lower socio-economic stratum struggle to bear the related expenses. Who benefits in the name of these rituals? The priests and their related grocers benefit. Birth is expensive, so is death, all because of these rituals, which have taken a more socio-religious dimension. Full compliance with such rituals has become a must for many for fear of social backlash and criticism. As for wealthier people, they get the opportunity to show off their wealth at these events, caught in some kind of rat race. Who benefits? Businesses benefit, the economy benefits, due to religious rituals.

No one loses except that poor person who finds it extremely hard to survive and make ends meet, but still goes into perpetual debt to comply socially and avoid shame. We therefore see religion is used to exploit people at every stage of social life for solely material benefit and in whose name? God! Who has seen God? No one! Why and how is God used for religious exploitation? Due to the fear of the unknown! Who cashes in? Priests!

Will materialism merge with spiritualism?

I believe materialism, catalysed by the light of scientific knowledge, will finally not only completely desensitise the human soul — and kill human consciousness — it may also get rid of the concepts of hell and heaven, and religious exploitation. It may seem to be a little oxymoronic but also I believe materialism will finally merge towards spiritualism. It has no other path to follow. I believe both are like yin and yang and complement, follow each other. Each pushes the other to some limit but only finds itself pushed back.

I believe a good, balanced life needs both spiritualism and materialism in equal measure. These lose relevance without the other. It is like good and bad. Both are relative and absurd without each other. Once this merger happens — initially on an individual level and gradually within entire communities — the traditional fears and beliefs that lack logic and scientific grounding will evaporate and disappear into ether. In the end, religion will become practically redundant; it has to, as there is no other recourse. Spiritualism will follow science, as both unify the world in their own ways. Both spiritualism and science help to bring out and promote humanism.

Chapter 12 THE TERRIFYING QUESTION

Man's obsession with death?

Vijay
When we repeatedly ask the question as to whether we took some wrong turns in the creation of our gods and beliefs, it is obviously in the context of the bitter acrimony and barbaric intolerance our religions still evoke. All of the best and highest attainments of our civilisations are negated by our wars of belief. Early humans sensed the existence of some powerful forces in Nature. In their wonder and fear, they looked for the force that was life — something that lived and moved and also fell to stillness in death. Life and fertility in Nature were worshipped very early in human history.

Phallic symbols and fertility rites and goddesses are known to have existed. The earliest religions and gods, animal and nature gods, and humanoid gods were to come later.

I think we can go to the main theme here in my mind. And it is that humans loved and worshipped life so much that they became obsessed with death. The entire focus of our religions has come to fall on death, and not life, in the sense that in many traditions, morality, worship and spiritual aspiration centres on what will happen to the individual after death. If we are to do good acts, it is to be rewarded with heaven or some other form of salvation. We must, the religions stipulate, be 'saved'. It is not always clear from what we are to be saved.

In Hinduism, there is a complete denial of life in the physical world and the goal of all religious practice and worship is to find an end, a release, from the cycle of birth and death that brings us to Earth. So the goal is *moksha* (freedom from, or the end of, life). I will not go too much into this, as we well know the Hindu ideas of an illusory world, the need to renounce and so on. This total denial of materialistic life had its repercussions in creating a passive, withdrawing society at a certain point in time. In today's India, we are seeing an explosion of crass materialism. I think this materialism underlines the fact that non-materialism and renunciatory beliefs were only a reaction to poverty.

Actually, I may venture to say that there was a denial of the physical body and its desires and passions in other religions too. In Christianity, we find a great emphasis on personal austerity and denial of physical pleasure, leading on to giving hardship, even pain to the body. This was true especially in the case of people in holy orders but I think there was certainly a kind of glorification of poverty and pain. In many Christian communities, people wore what was called a cilice, which was made of coarse cloth or animal hair, sometimes even of wire or chain. This was worn next to the skin so as to cause irritation and pain that was seen as repentance, a form of worship. Such a glorification was to be found also in Hinduism and Islam. The Hindu ascetics are known for their self-torture and practice of extreme poverty, and there is self-flagellation in cults of Islam and historically in Christianity too. Giving pain to the body, and living in hardship and poverty, was supposed to please the various gods who would then bestow immortality or salvation (*Moksha*).

Living and how to live in the material and physical world was dealt within commandments and moral codes. But the emphasis then and now is on the 'higher matters' — the afterlife, oneness with God, immortality and salvation. The higher matters are in the realm of speculation, philosophy and imagination. The 'lower matters' are the body and the senses, the mind as it deals with the world, Nature and the environment in which we live, and patterns of behaviour with people. To live well and at your best level, these have to be understood.

Bill
I knew it was coming, Vijay — the fear of death and the unknown afterlife. Well, as you know, humans can't reconcile to the idea that there is nothing after death. To create our imagined immortality and the continuity of our existence, we created heaven and hell. These had

Chapter 12 THE TERRIFYING QUESTION

multiple uses. Not only did it allow us to believe we were immortal, but it also allowed us to send our opponents to hell once they died naturally or were killed. We also created heaven for ourselves where we could enjoy bliss as long we followed our religion.

When things don't turn out exactly as we expect, despite praying to God or performing rituals — some quite bizarre, including inflicting pain on ourselves — some of us become disillusioned, some temporarily and others permanently. When some people turn away from their faith after it fails to materially repay their devotion, they either turn into atheists or convert to a different faith that promises more material benefits or something that attracts them.

Many people in prison convert to a faith from having none or being atheist?. In all cases, what they are promised is material in nature, and all those material rewards are available and delivered right here in this life and on the Earth.

When some of us are talked back into the folds of our religion — under the drivers of Karma, Destiny or simply the will of God — in no case is God blamed or held guilty or deemed impotent. Either it is our Karma or Destiny. Investment in religion is very popular among many people of faith, like an insurance policy. Gemstones in finger rings are also prescribed to reap those rich material dividends. Sadly, no one is able to see the dividends that are promised after death, as no one comes back from the dead to tell the story. Who has seen the promised heaven?

Many people torture themselves or others and make great sacrifices — of others or themselves — for the promise of redemption or heaven after death or to absolve themselves of sin, as defined in or inferred from religious texts. How sad it would be if we come to know after some time that there was actually no afterlife or heaven or hell or Karma or Destiny! What kind of losers would we feel like if we realised our biological existence was nothing different to that of worms and insects?

Heaven and hell both have material uses. In spiritualism, there are no hells or heavens, all is here and now.

Religions lose their spiritual aspects

Vijay
From the time the major, more important religions of the world became organised, they took a direction that would drag them away from their main purpose. I would bring to you the words of Swami Vivekananda: 'Religion has only one purpose and that is to guide man towards God. Religion has no business to interfere in other things.'

But as it turned out, every system of faith, though it started with a philosophy of man and God or Divinity, went headlong into social and personal behaviour, sin and retribution, rituals and ceremonies and doctrines of belief. The pure spiritual element was lost. This could also have been because the masses of ordinary humans did not really want pure spirituality of a personal kind from religion.

Those who do find spirituality find it by themselves in every faith, sometimes even without a system of faith. For the rest, religion is only a way to ask God for something — a shortcut to wish fulfilment. Or it is a system of rituals and ceremonies for the milestones of life. Churches and temples are also places for social events.

There are also people who are very serious about salvation and oneness with God or in ensuring a place in heaven. The religions were very clever to cater to all these demands. With larger congregations, they also meant more wealth and power.

The original and primeval idea of experiencing the highest levels of human life and the Divinity that humans felt in moments of epiphany was lost. Religion became a source of social morality, it interfered in politics and rulership and governments, and it came across as another system of the physical, materialistic world.

It was a moment of outrage and horror to eighteenth-century Europe

Chapter 12 THE TERRIFYING QUESTION

when the philosopher Nietzsche announced that 'God is dead'. He also said that disbelief in religion and God would create a period of chaos and nihilism since man would not have the anchor of belief. But this was necessary, he thought, and man would have to face this vacuum before he could think for himself and work out his own meaning and purpose in life. Nietzsche was right and also wrong, I think. He was right that there would be a kind of nihilism in the absence of religion and god beliefs. But he was wrong about the chaos.

Generations of post-war people have experienced disbelief in traditional morality, class structures and religious dogma. Lo and behold the human propensity to change and embrace the new and survive: since the 1950s up until now, there have been many spiritual movements, the rise of what we call New Spirituality. There have been millions of people going over to rational philosophies of existentialism, even to agnosticism and atheism and so on.

People have found other ways. There is more free thinking now than ever before. People are questioning and doubting and also going overboard with scientific knowledge. It is possible also to see religions changing or coming up in newer forms in the future. I say this with the awareness that religions today are very strong, powerful institutions and will not give in easily to change. Yet I believe history as it happens always surprises us. There has always been change in religions as they have branched into other religions and sects. Three great religions of Buddhism, Jainism and Sikhism came with some of the core beliefs of Hinduism. There are dozens of sects of Hinduism, as of Christianity and Islam, each claiming to be true, perfect and authentic.

Buddhism in its original ancient form changed to Zen Buddhism as it travelled to China and Japan. And the core Hindu philosophy of *Advaita* (monism) became a central belief in modern Zen. So we see that even the religions changing their form and adapting to the changing world, as their rigidity can potentially work against their survival and render them practically irrelevant. Even the gods sometimes have an expiry date as new gods come up. The endless flux affects the materialistic as well as the spiritual world.

I think it was you, Bill, who just said in this discussion that it would be terrible for a pious person who practised dire austerities or even tortured themselves to find that they got it wrong, that what they were doing had no traction in the spiritual quest for meaning. The meaning is all here in your life and it is the individual who gives meaning to themselves. I think that is a basic truth that more and more people are realising now.

Bill

I am sharing what a seventeen-year old student from Hyderabad wrote to me last night. We must consider his thoughts. He represents our future. I think his thoughts must find space in this book, which has created itself for future generations. India is changing, from a quintessential all-embracing Hindu India to a more assertive and self-discovering Hindu nation, thanks to the *Hindutva* ideology, encouraged by the current government. On the current conditions in India, he said:

'I feel, even though our country was "told" to follow secularism, we have always partitioned ourselves based on similarity of thoughts, emotions and feelings. To come unto an agreement on the definition and understanding of our sacred body; our surroundings; our purpose in life and the set of rules to be followed during our tenure, holy texts were written in different languages and perspectives with the intent to convey the same meaning to the people following different religions. This led to the formation of diverse ethical ancestral perspectives, viewpoints from different walks of life. Holy texts were a little misinterpreted and are understood in the wrong way, which cause the problems in India, Sir.

'The Constitution (Indian Constitution) was never given importance while considering the aggregate population of our nation. I think the one and only form of pure and realistic categorisation is *religion*.

Chapter 12 THE TERRIFYING QUESTION

That is the reason it was able to sustain the evolution of humans over the past centuries.

'Religion is a powerful word, which acts like a bridge between us and the universe (God) and it shouldn't be contemplated as a barricade for a prosperous nation. Principles set in each religion are meant to unify our country but not divide us. There has to be secularism in one's individual actions but we cannot allow it to define the status of a country. Our Constitution is slowing our growth with all the rules and regulations copied from various other books that are not valid in India, Sir.'

I advised this young lad: 'Keep your thoughts independent and pure, nourish them with good books from around the world.'

Vijay
I think it is good that you shared it here. I think it is a point of view of a youngster who is obviously conditioned by all inputs that a youngster normally gets from family and society. I would be surprised if it was different. There are millions who think this way.

These are not Western standards. They are universal human standards. Freedom, love, inclusiveness, liberalism, equality and fraternity are for *every human*. Neither religion nor politics nor local culture can be higher than these. Of course, he is a religious follower and thinks it is powerful. There are billions on Earth who swear by religion and there will always be such people. Religion does not unite and we have enough evidence of that.

And it is not a misrepresentation of holy books; for example, Manusmriti is in front of us, endorsing caste and the suppression of women. So does the Koran endorse inhuman treatment of women, death to kafirs and jihad. Christianity endorsed the taking of slaves. And that it is how religion was used. The Vatican financed Hitler and endorsed extermination of Jews. So that is it. It is not a matter of he is right and we are wrong. What is right and true? What is the reality?

- What has religion done in India?
- Why do we need categorisation of religion?
- Why is it not that we are just humans?

No, this is just the usual thinking of people who support this potential holocaust. Do you know they have built detention camps here for 1.9 million people? How do they get to that number and how did they decide it? Human values are not Indian or American or Australian. They are universal. That is a given, not negotiable. All this about holy tests and so on, and we were '"told" to follow secularism' is the conditioning of a young mind. It is there. And all these 'holy' texts were written by men, as a rule. There can be no rules that oppress the individual.

No, Bill, this is not the future. It is the recycling of India's past in young minds. It is not that Bill Koul and Vijay Shankar are saying egotistically that what we say is right and true. All people of thought and humanistic universal values have said it and are dying for it in different ways. Well, there it is.

Bill

Vijay, you may have again hit the nail right on its head. Humans are social animals, trying to satisfy their hunger and thirst through all the five senses. Some satisfied souls, however, have also altruistic needs and are drawn towards spirituality. But spirituality, as such, is generally seen as an unattractive, absurd and theoretical concept. It does not suit the palate of the common person who is driven by hedonistic needs. People can't just reconcile with the spiritual concept of 'nothing' and 'nothingness'. That is where religion comes in to satisfy those needs.

In essence, where spirituality binds and elevates humans above manmade division, connecting them with not only one another but also with everything around them – their environment and all other life forms – religion has unfortunately been used, by religious and political leaders, to divide them and confine them within separate silos.

Chapter 12 THE TERRIFYING QUESTION

Our hedonic needs have become our weaknesses, which have been exploited by opportunists. We have been paying for our weaknesses and we shall always keep paying. In our relationship with God, many of us trust the brokers and middlemen of religions, who also have not met or seen God. Amazingly, not many people realise that, if these brokers and middlemen of religions can't help themselves, how can they possibly help others. Not many people are able to digest the fact that these brokers too are prone to sicknesses, diseases and accidents, and mere mortals.

Religions survive and prosper due to their promise of material rewards, which are visible or can be imagined. It is their material aspects that perhaps keep them alive and exposed to surreptitious exploitation by religious gurus and politicians. In India, pilgrims and temple-goers donate vast amounts of cash and gold to famous temples and shrines, and gurus. Why? Can those donations be deemed as attempts to bribe God? Like any other monetary transaction, the donors too expect material rewards and successes in return. These dominations are also made as thanks-giving to God after a certain reward or success has been received. Generally, people pray (and pay) for good health, wealth, house, promotion, admission, wedding and birth of children, especially male children. The Hindu prayer (*Arti*), *Om Jai Jagdish Hare*, is immersed in want for materialistic rewards. Remove the material aspects of a religion and see how it collapses right before your eyes.

Buddhism was almost routed out of India because it is essentially atheistic and lacks the material aspects of Hinduism, such as God's presence and that God is sitting high above in the sky on a throne and rewards us with material benefits in exchange for our prayers and donations at temples and to priests, finally allocating us a place in heaven after we die. Islam too provides attractive material benefits and facilities in heaven to the faithful, especially the martyrs who die fighting jihad.

Many people also tend to get disillusioned with religion when God is found to be missing, for example, in the following scenarios, and, as a reaction, either turn to atheism and / or spiritualism without following any particular religion:

- Despite having strong faith and making regular hefty monetary donations to temples and deities, people don't get rewarded materially in return.
- During natural calamities – cyclones, flood, drought, earthquake, Tsunami, bushfire – where habitats are destroyed and many people die or get uprooted.
- During war when numerous innocent people – children, women and older people – get killed or maimed in bombings carried out by the opposing forces.
- When perceived 'good' seems to consistently lose to perceived 'evil'.
- When people suffer and die of disease, hunger and poverty due to relentless exploitation by wealthy and the powerful.
- When babies, children and women are abused, raped and killed by adults, sometimes by their own flesh and blood.
- When people are systemically mistreated, prejudiced and marginalised by mighty and influential people.

[Incidentally, the countries that have predominantly atheistic populations — Japan and Australia — also have relatively lower crime rates and social strife.]

Spirituality binds one to Nature

When we say religion was meant to link us with God, we are being overly simplistic in our assumption. God has not been seen to be loved. God is generally prayed for insurance, just in case, mainly because of the fear factor – fear of the unknown – and, of course, the rewards. On the contrary, Nature is benevolent, non-discriminatory, all-giving and opens arms to everyone — the good, bad and the ugly — every being that exists out there.

Most people belonging to religions don't see Nature as God. If only humans could see Nature as God, they would see their image in the other person, stop fighting in the name of God and religion, and embrace one another. To me, that is spirituality.

The world would be coherent, peaceful and, therefore, sustainable. But we humans have even misused science and technology, which has otherwise made our lives so comfortable. We have developed a large range of weapons of mass destruction that has the potential to destroy life on Earth several times over. We have not learnt from Nature.

In conclusion, I reiterate my firm belief that, as the world population increases and capitalism flourishes, materialism will potentially kill human consciousness. That would be the lowest point of evolution in our human existence. After that, oxymoronic as it may sound, I believe materialism will start merging with spiritualism, as it has no other path; they have been pushing each other for a long time and have no relevance without each other. Upon their merging, the traditional fears about hell and heaven, and beliefs that lack scientific grounding will disappear. In the end, religion will most likely become practically redundant; it has to, as there is no other recourse. Spiritualism will continue to follow science and that is logical, as both unify the world and help to promote humanism. And that is truth. *Satyamev Jayte* — Truth alone triumphs!

www.ingramcontent.com/pod-product-compliance
Lightning Source LLC
Chambersburg PA
CBHW032041090426
42744CB00004B/85